The Place Names of Historic

SLEEPY HOLLOW

&

TARRYTOWN

Henry Steiner

HERITAGE BOOKS
2008

HERITAGE BOOKS
AN IMPRINT OF HERITAGE BOOKS, INC.

Books, CDs, and more—Worldwide

For our listing of thousands of titles see our website at
www.HeritageBooks.com

Published 2008 by
HERITAGE BOOKS, INC.
Publishing Division
100 Railroad Ave. #104
Westminster, Maryland 21157

Copyright © 1998 Henry Steiner

All rights reserved. No part of this book may be reproduced or transmitted in any form or by any means, electronic or mechanical, including photocopying, recording or by any information storage and retrieval system without written permission from the author, except for the inclusion of brief quotations in a review.

International Standard Book Numbers
Paperbound: 978-0-7884-0961-5
Clothbound: 978-0-7884-7131-5

"A man must generally get away some hundreds or thousands of miles from home before he can be said to begin his travels. Why not begin his travels at home? Would he have to go far or look very closely to discover novelties?"

—*Thoreau*

This book is dedicated with love to my mother, Lucie O. Steiner.

Table of Contents

Page#

Introduction----------------------------------3
Authors Note--------------------------------7

Place Names

Beginning with "A"----------------------------8
Beginning with "B"----------------------------18
Beginning with "C"----------------------------30
Beginning with "D"----------------------------43
Beginning with "E"----------------------------48
Beginning with "F"----------------------------50
Beginning with "G"----------------------------53
Beginning with "H"----------------------------58
Beginning with "I"----------------------------65
Beginning with "J"----------------------------67
Beginning with "K"----------------------------70
Beginning with "L"----------------------------74
Beginning with "M"----------------------------79
Beginning with "N"----------------------------86
Beginning with "O"----------------------------89
Beginning with "P"----------------------------94
Beginning with "Q-R"--------------------------112
Beginning with "S"----------------------------119
Beginning with "T"----------------------------135
Beginning with "U"----------------------------147
Beginning with "V"----------------------------149
Beginning with "W"----------------------------150
Beginning with "Y"----------------------------155
Beginning with "Z"----------------------------157

Bibliography---------------------------------158
About the Author-----------------------------175

Captors' Monument
The statue is said to depict John Paulding. Photo by Henry Steiner.

Introduction

The names attached to places, landmarks, topographical features can remind us that a given place had a function or significance before our time. Place names lend character to the landscape and stand as milestones to history. They can be elusive too. They change, get displaced, and fade from use.

Place names often evolve through an accident of speech or writing. They are commonly created to identify, describe, or memorialize a place. Some place names are universally accepted, others are known only to a few. I prefer to believe that place names do not die, they merely fall from fashion—somewhere amid a tangle of modern highways lies Youngs' Corners, a place frozen in history where ancient, now invisible roads meet. There Loyalist troops sought out their rebellious Whig enemies, engaged them in deadly combat, and there they lie entombed in peace.

Place names can demonstrate a remarkable wanderlust. Few realize that the name Westchester was adopted from a town which stood in what is today the Bronx (then the county seat of Westchester County). The upstate New York names of Utica, Rome, Ithaca, and Syracuse are obvious examples of place names on-the-move.

Some place names refer to vague and amorphous geographical areas, others to concretely defined boundaries. A modern example of a loosely defined place name is that portion of the Hudson River shore in the Village of Sleepy Hollow known as the Yellow Rocks, or simply Yellow Rocks. It is difficult to say exactly where that particular place begins and ends. Yellow Rocks is also a good example of a place name for which written references are quite rare; but in some Native American form it could be the oldest place name in the two villages.

The place names, Village of North Tarrytown (now the Village of Sleepy Hollow) and Village of Tarrytown, are very specific. They are creations of the 1870s when the two municipalities were incorporated. They refer to well-described locations and boundaries, unlike earlier place names for these communities.

In the late eighteenth century, Tarrytown, was not a "village" incorporated under the laws of New York State, but a hamlet—amorphous in its shape and extent. At that time the place name Tarrytown referred to a settled nucleus with indistinct boundaries. The exact limits of early Tarrytown are subject to interpretation and vary with time. A cow standing by the Pocantico River might be described as being "in Tarrytown" or "near Tarrytown" depending on how the reporter interpreted the place name.

The name Tarrytown began as a reference to a central district or a cluster of buildings. By contrast, today's Village of Tarrytown describes the precise geographic limits of the municipality. In Revolutionary times the name Tarrytown applied to a center, "at Tarrytown," but the name also furnished a convenient way to identify outlying lands associated with the quiet hamlet—these places were said to be "near Tarrytown," "by Tarrytown," "at Tarrytown," "Tarrytown." The pre-1870 name, Tarrytown, is an important local place name, and a difficult one to define.

When I travel past long familiar places in and around the villages of Sleepy Hollow and Tarrytown, I am fond of remarking, "This is where I used to go to get in trouble when I was a kid." Trouble was never far from home, and the places where I could find it seemed limitless. We were a group of boys who lived on Crest Drive near the cul-de-sac which we called "the Circle." Our forays to find trouble took us anywhere from Axe Castle to Catfish Pond. Very close at hand was Lemonade Rock, further off was Hackley Pond (by the old shooting range, not far from the site of the old stables). Down between the Lakes and the old Marymount Secondary School was Marymount Pond. Did anyone else call these features by the same names, or had we invented them? We all knew where Catfish Pond was (as do many other residents of the two villages), but I have yet to see the name on a map or in a book. Later on, in adolescent years, with a somewhat different team of comrades, the allure of trouble called from Pennybridge to the very boundaries of Rockwood Hall.

One of my reasons for writing this book is to help preserve the old names. Some of them can be found only in fragile limited editions more than a century old. It is a sad fact that the work of collecting and preserving local documents is often pursued with scant resources.

This means that irreplaceable records are constantly threatened with extinction due to a lack of time, money, and interest.

I hope this collection will also serve as a source book for local research. Efforts in local research and preservation are often interrupted by long periods of inactivity, and valuable work is easily lost. This can make it difficult for those conducting research to pick up the thread of earlier efforts. Since many of the local histories of the nineteenth century do not offer source information, it can be a painstaking or impossible task to judge their accuracy. My hope is that the references to be found in this work will make it easier for those interested in local history to locate, evaluate, and interpret some of the old source material.

In addition to place names within Sleepy Hollow and Tarrytown, I have included names of some places and features which extend through and beyond the two villages, such as roads, rivers, hills, and townships. Also listed are some significant place names which denote places near the two villages.

In the case of private estates, it may be hard to say whether a name applies to a place, to a mansion, or to both. In such cases I have generally taken the view that the name applies at least to the place, as in Sunnyside, Lyndhurst, Carrollwood. (Some modern books dealing with local architecture may lead the reader to assume that these names apply only to the dwellings, since that is the main focus of discussion.) With important exceptions, names of streets and man-made structures have been excluded from this compilation.

I have looked for the earliest occurrence of a given name, but I know that many have eluded me. A place name can be in use for a long time before it is recorded in even the most transient fashion. In many cases I have attempted to trace the derivation of names. Also included are variations. Local names adopted from languages other than English tend to show up in an interesting variety of forms. Names of natural features are included—rivers, hills, boulders, trees, and valleys. For some interesting background information on street names, please see Canning and Buxton [CA], pages 198 - 206.

I regret that in compiling these names I have not been able to speak with more of my neighbors in Sleepy Hollow and Tarrytown. There are certainly many more names to be gleaned from the "remembered record." Although a collection of this sort will never be complete, I hope that in time, more of our local place names will be gathered up.

The published work of dedicated local historians past and present was invaluable to me in compiling this book. Also indispensable was the help of numerous librarians and curators at Warner Library, Westchester County Historical Society, New York Public Library, New York Historical Society, Historical Society of the Tarrytowns, and residents of the two villages, past and present.

A special note of appreciation goes to several friends. Christopher Skelly has offered encouragement throughout the process. Writer Staci Swedeen made valuable suggestions about the book's format. Innumerable contributions to the manuscript were made by my wife, Judith Rohan Steiner; I could not have completed this work without her generous help.

H. S.

Sleepy Hollow
November 1997

A note on the format of this book

This work is partly intended to provide a framework for further study. For this reason references and a bibliography are provided. A place name is followed by commentary, then variations (if any), and then a list of reference codes. The codes refer to the corresponding bibliographic entries. Codes from books and other texts are followed by a colon, then a page reference. Where appropriate, a volume number is also included. Each reference is separated by a semicolon. These reference codes refer either to occurrences of a place name or to some aspect of the commentary. An attempt has been made to supply references for at least several instances of a name.

Entries for place names which lie entirely outside the vllages of Sleepy Hollow and Tarrytown are followed by an asterisk.

Key to Map

1. Rockefeller State Park Preserve
2. Sleepy Hollow Cemetery
   (formerly Tarrytown Cemetery)
3. Battle Hill
4. Philipse Manor Station
   (Hudson Valley Writers' Center)
5. Old Dutch Church
   (of Sleepy Hollow)
6. Sleepy Hollow Bridge
   (Headless Horseman Bridge)
7. Sleepy Hollow
8. Philipsburg Manor—Upper Mills
9. Kykuit Hill
   (formerly Davids' Hill)
10. Kingsland Point
    (formerly Beekman Point)
11. Tarrytown Lighthouse
12. General Motors Site
    (formerly Slapershaven)
13. Captors' Monument
14. Tarrytown Lakes
15. Depot Plaza
    (formerly Tarrytown Bay)
16. Tappan Hill
17. Tarry Crest
18. Lyndhurst
    (formerly Paulding Manor)
19. Sunnyside

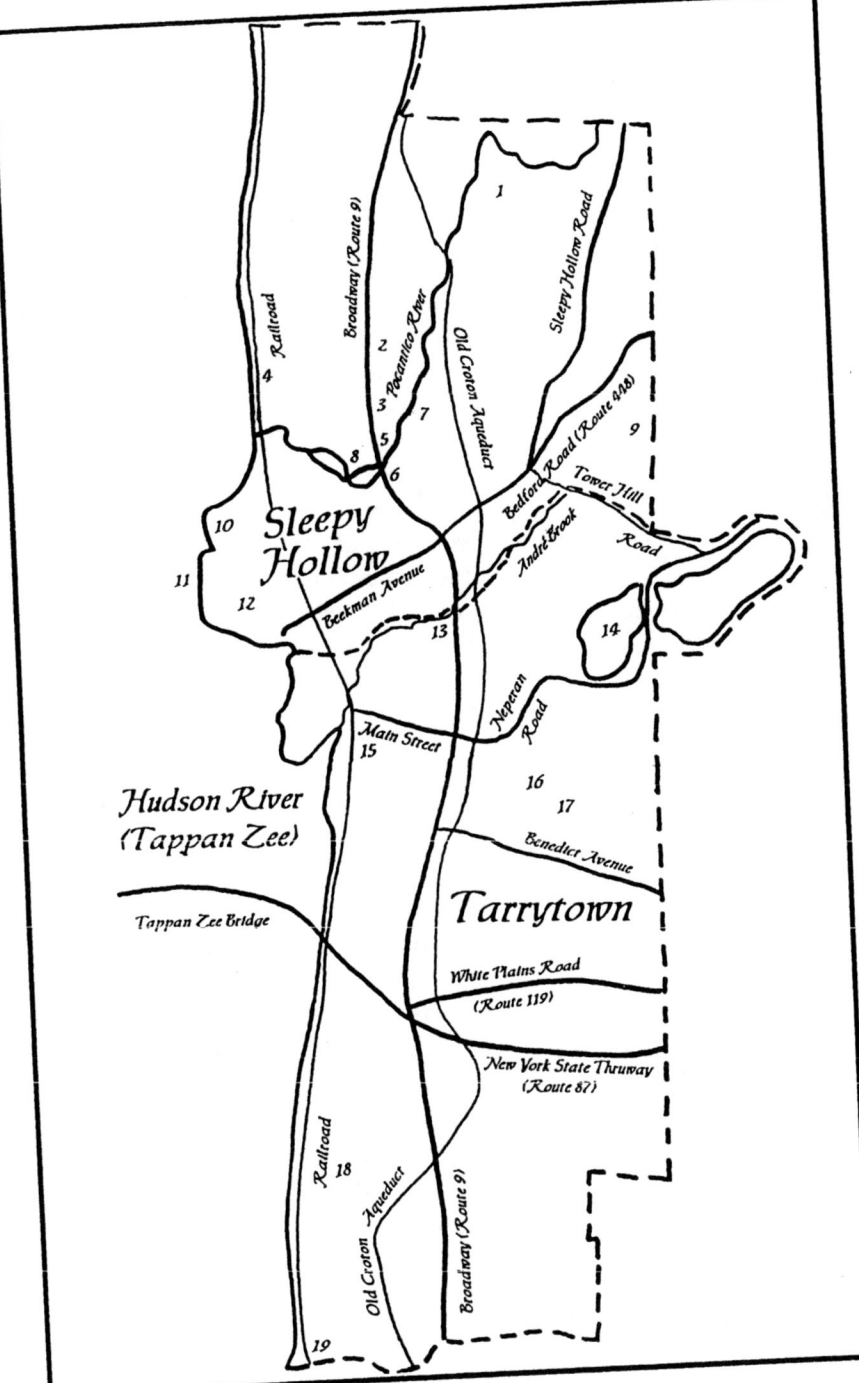

Abram Storm Brook

A local surveyor and long-time village resident, George Carpenter, contributed a series of articles to the *Tarrytown Argus* newspaper [AR] in 1882. In it he wrote of a small brook which ran along present day Central Avenue in Tarrytown. The brook was known as Abram Storm Brook or Mekeel Brook. At least one old map [M38] shows a brook at this location. The stream emptied into André Brook near the southeast corner of Cortlandt Street and Wildey Street. Canning [CA] notes that in the early 1900s there was a small reservoir near the corner of Central Avenue and Kaldenberg Place.

Abram Storm Brook appears to have been the southern boundary of the 327 acre farm purchased by Michael Mekeel after the Revolution. [See the Couzens Map [M1].]] Mekeel's land was north of John Van Tassel's farm. The presence of this stream and water source may explain the location of the Van Tassel Tavern (Jacob Mott House) nearby. André Brook lay to the north of the Mekeel farm. The farm extended eastward to where the Tarrytown Lakes are today.

See Wilson Park, Jacob Mott House.

REF: AR [Apr. 1 1882]; CA:95; M1; M38; SC:232.

Albany Post Road, the

The route which is still occasionally referred to as the Albany Post Road passes through the villages of Tarrytown and Sleepy Hollow on its course from New York City to Albany. Today villagers more commonly refer to this route as Broadway or Route 9. The road has had other names: the Highland Turnpike, the King's Highway, the Queen's Highway.

In 1703, the building and maintenance of this highway, so important to local history, was authorized by the general assembly of the Province of New York. In 1704 and 1705, two more acts pertaining to highways were passed by the assembly and communicated by the English Governor, Cornbury, to the Lords of Trade in London. It appears that the improved road was completed through Irvington by about 1723.

The act of 1703, cited in Hine [HI], states that the highway was to have a breadth of "four rods, English measurement, at the least." Some say that this highway was actually a refinement of earlier paths established by settlers, American Indians, and even wild animals which traveled along the most convenient ground near and more or less parallel to the Hudson. Jenkins [JE] writes that a post road was open between New York and Yonkers in 1669.

The route of the Albany Post Road through the two villages has changed over the centuries. South of the Warner Library, the route appears to have changed but little. North of the library it has changed significantly, and there is a good deal of disagreement among authorities as to where, when, and why.

Any discussion of where the road previously ran through Sleepy Hollow must be related to a specific time in order to have relevance. In the Revolutionary period, the road appears to have deviated from its present day path north of the Warner Library. It seems to have veered up the hillside to the west side of Paulding School; the road then declined gradually back down the hillside toward the west side of the Korean Church (formerly the First Reformed Church). From here it ran a short distance along what is today New Broadway, then down through present day Webber Park, crossing the Pocantico about seventy-five to one hundred yards upstream of the present Route 9 bridge. From here the route swung abruptly in a kind of "S" curve southwest along the Pocantico towards Philipse Castle. It turned north where Route 9 runs today, continuing north past the Old Dutch Church on the west side, approximating its route today. [See the important survey of Erskine [M12] dating from this period. Also see M33 and M6.] It appears that substantial changes were made to the André Brook and Webber Park portions of the route during the building of the first Croton Aqueduct (Old Croton Aqueduct).

Note that one modern local history [CA] records that the road passed to the east of the Old Dutch Church until about 1837. This is clearly incorrect; in fact, there appears to be little evidence that the post road, at any time, passed to the east of the church as several twentieth century sources have reported.

The road is labeled as *Chemin d'Albany* in a French map of the Battle of White Plains [M15]. See Scharf [SC] for an interesting discussion of the farms which lined the Post Road before 1800. Also, see Raymond's account of this route during the Revolutionary War in

Washington at Tarrytown [RAY].
VAR: Albany post road, old Albany Post Road, the Post Road, Old Post Road, Albany-New York Road, Albany Post-road, Albany post-road, US Route 9, the Queen's Road; Chemin d'Albany, hiland [sic] Turnpike.
REF: *ABB:28; BA:138; BOL:vol.I,274; CA:47,206; DA2 [Mar. 12 1937], [Oct. 10 1942]; DU:8; HAND:23,24; HI:1,2,6; HU:46,52,53; JE:343-346,381; M6; M12; M17; M22; M33[COL:129]; M31; M51; M52; M57; MI:9; OC:[vol.4]1065, 1114,1168; OW:20; PE1: vol.24/3 326; PH:np; PHI:np; PHIL:np; TA:map; TAP:np; TN [Oct. 31 1996]; TW:12; WI:142; WO:12; YE:np.*

Alipconck

The Delaware Indian name, Alipconck, is said to mean "the place of the elms," or "where the elms grow." As is often the case with place names in translation, we find many variations of spelling and pronunciation.

This is one of the oldest recorded names in the villages of Sleepy Hollow and Tarrytown. Alipconck was an American Indian village which reportedly stood near the old mouth of the Pocantico, near the General Motors site. Others say it stood further south, near the foot of Church Street, close to the site of a Revolutionary War earthwork. There, shell deposits, also known as "oyster kitches," were clearly visible in the nineteenth century [BOL]. These are generally believed to indicate early American Indian settlement. Another oyster kitch is still visible on the hillside above the Yellow Rocks in Sleepy Hollow.

Still other sources suggest that, since the American Indian inhabitants of this area were chiefly migratory, there was no village or settlement per se. Statements regarding Native American life in this locale should be related to a specific time-frame since American Indian habitation of the area may have spanned more than two millennia. The native people living in the area of the two villages during the advent of the Dutch were Weckquaesgecks, a tribe of the Delawares. Some say that this tribe was part of the Wappinger confederacy which aligned with the Mohegans of southwest Connecticut. The Weckquaesgeck Hudson River lands were located in the Sleepy Hollow-Tarrytown-Irvington-Dobbs Ferry area. Alipconck seems to have been the smaller of two Hudson River settlements of the Weckquaesgecks. The larger one was situated in Dobbs Ferry. To the north were the Sink

Sinks and to the south, the Rechgawawanks of Yonkers and the Bronx.

Delawares referred to themselves as Lenape or Leni-Lenape, which means "original people." They held a special status among other Algonquin tribes due to their antiquity. The Delawares employed the Munsee and Unami languages, both eastern Algonquian tongues. At the time of the European intrusion, tribes of the Delaware language group inhabited the region from the Delaware River to the lower Hudson River Valley. Those of the Lower Hudson generally used the Munsee tongue. There were said to be eleven Munsee-speaking tribes on the lower Hudson in the days of New Amsterdam.

Adrian Van der Donck recorded detailed contemporary information regarding the culture of the Hudson River's Native Americans in his work, *Beschryvinge Van Nieuw Nederlant* [DAN]. These people lived by hunting, fishing, cultivating beans and corn, and gathering chestnuts. Through the mid-1600s their custom was to occupy forts and "castles" during the winter months, spending the warm months growing crops at their riverside villages. In some cases their castles enclosed as many as twenty or thirty houses. In summer, it was their custom to journey *en mass* to the seashore to gather shellfish, particularly clams and oysters. These, according to Van der Donck, "they know how to dry, and preserve good a long time." In the warm months they cultivated gardens. After the harvest would come their main ceremonial season. They foraged for nuts, berries, and roots; cornmeal mush was also a staple.

The tribes of this region kept the forests open by burning the underbrush in late fall. In that season they hunted in large parties, driving game into blind enclosures for slaughter. Their game included raccoons, wolves, deer, fishes, weasels, turkeys, and otters. Shad, eel, sturgeon, striped bass, and other local species were taken from the Hudson and its tributaries.

The Weckquaesgecks dressed lightly, even in winter; men wore a breech-cloth and women an unsewed overlapping skirt. After the arrival of the Dutch, they commonly took to wearing a knotted blanket over the shoulder. Males might wear a loose, untucked shirt. They used belts, deer-skin moccasins, wampum, and copper jewelry. Their skin was often adorned with paint and tattoos, or protected with animal grease.

Communal long-houses measured about twenty feet by one

hundred feet, and were covered in bark; a hole in the roof allowed smoke to escape. Clay pots and gourd water bottles were used, as well as rush mats, pipes of clay or horn, stone axes, and hoes. Their arrowheads, usually shaped in triangular fashion, were made of stone, horn, or bone. Bows were five to six feet long and strung with braided sinew. The Delawares also used small elm-bark canoes, pine candles, and reed flutes.

In war, combatants would arm themselves with clubs, wooden helmets, and large rectangular shields. Captives were subject to torture, execution, and scalping.

In 1643, a large number of Weckquaesgecks, seeking protection from hostile tribes to the north, were massacred by the Dutch near New Amsterdam. This ignited two years of bloody warfare between the Dutch and the tribes of the lower Hudson Valley.

Early Westchester County historian Robert Bolton [BO] indicates that a Weckquaesgeck fort and burying ground stood on the hillside where the Old Dutch Church of Sleepy Hollow was later to be built. Bolton also writes that there were still many Indians living along the banks of the Hudson in the area of Tarrytown in 1755.

The name, Alipconck, is occasionally found in the contemporary records of New Netherlands. An early incidence of the name appears on a map accompanying the 1656 Dutch edition of Van der Donck's *A Description of the New Netherlands*. This is Visscher's map, *Norum Belgium*.

See also Weckquaesgeck.

VAR: *Alipconk, Alipkonck, Alipkonek, Alipkonk, Aliponck, Aliponeck, Anneebikong?*

REF: BOL:vol.I,259,260,294; CA:16,198; CON:5,24,map; COR:np; DA2 [Mar. 12 1937]; DE:2GR:51; HAN:213-239; HI:19; JE:372,381; LE:8; LOS:185; M10; M17; M57; MO:1; ODC:47; OW:6; RO:6; SC:199; SH:25,46; ST; TA:6 ; TAR:1; TWO:47; VA:4,74-82.

Alipconck Brook

This brook is mentioned in the *Tarrytown Argus* of April 22, 1882. George Carpenter, citing the deed of Gerard Beekman, refers to "Holmes or Alipconck Brook."

See Alipconck, Holmes Brook.

REF: AR [Apr. 22 1882].

André Brook
At Patriots Park. Captors' Monument can be seen top right. Photo by Henry Steiner.

Anderson Park

This name refers to the former estate of nineteenth century millionaire tobacconist, John Anderson. It was of roughly the same extent as today's Webber Park and Douglas Park together. Anderson was a successful businessman, a philanthropist, a supporter of the Italian leader, Garibaldi, and a generous sponsor of improvements to the Captors' Monument in Patriots Park. [See Captors' Monument.]

According to a contemporary newspaper, Anderson started out as a mason and bricklayer. He resided in Tarrytown for a few years about 1860 and returned to the area in 1872.

Anderson died in 1880 while abroad. His Sleepy Hollow estate was purchased in 1886 by one of his legal executors, John Webber. It is not clear exactly when the area was called Anderson Park, but it was likely between the tenures of Anderson and Webber.

See Sleepy Hollow Park, Douglas Park, and Webber Park.

REF: AR [Nov. 26 1881]; CA:200,288,289; HUFE:82; M37; TN [Oct. 31 1996].

André Brook

This rivulet runs along the common boundary of the two incorporated villages of Sleepy Hollow and Tarrytown; therefore, it is also a shared boundary of the townships of Mount Pleasant and Greenburgh. The brook once marked the southern border of the post-Revolutionary Beekman Farm. It also represented the southern extent of lands associated with the Upper Mills, leased by William Pugsley in 1761 from Frederick Philipse III.

The stream is named for the capture of Major John André. André served as adjutant-general to the supreme commander of the British army in North America, Sir Henry Clinton. He was captured by three young American militiamen on September 22, 1780. These area natives stopped André at gunpoint as he was crossing the stream on horseback. The British officer was a key player in the treason of American General Benedict Arnold, and he was traveling in disguise with confidential plans to the American stronghold at West Point which had been given to him by Arnold. As a result of his capture, André was tried before an American court martial and hanged as a spy at Tappan, New York, on October 2, 1780.

There is some disagreement as to exactly where the capture took place. It certainly occurred close to the brook at its intersection with the Revolutionary Post Road. Based on Erskine's survey [M12], which was completed in the time of the capture, this intersection was located near the front entrance of today's Paulding Elementary School. (Present day Broadway is about one hundred yards further west at its intersection with André Brook.) In fact, according to information in the survey [M12] and Abbott [ABB], Bedford Road intersected with the Post Road immediately north of Andre Brook during the Revolution. In other words, at that time, Bedford Road paralleled the brook down to the Post Road, much different from its course today.

The brook begins at Kykuit Hill and empties into the Hudson at Tarrytown Bay. In the mid-nineteenth century, students at Newman's Tarrytown Academy (also known as the Tarrytown Institute), located at the corner of Broadway and College Avenue, occasionally used the stream for bathing. It is evident from Bolton [BO], the name André Brook was in common usage by 1848 or earlier. About 1876, the brook was used briefly as a public water supply. A pumping station at Wildey and Washington Streets forced water into a reservoir at Rose Hill, but the water quality was poor.

Before it was called André Brook, the stream was known as Clark's Kill. James K. Paulding [PA:109] describes Clark's Kill as being approximately half a mile north of the Martin Smith Tavern, at the corner of Main Street and the Post Road.

See a separate entry for Clark's Kill, also André's Tree, and Captors' Monument.

VAR: André's Brook, The André Brook, Andre Brook.
REF: ABB:28; BA:Map; BACO:14; BO:213; BOL:vol.I,308; CA:39; HA:72; HU:105; IN:57; LE:8; LO:330; LOS:196-206; M1; M3; M12; M17; M20:22; M21; M42; M45; M65; MI:1; OW:20; P5; PA:109; RO:5; SC:205; TAR:22; TARR:np; TN [Oct. 2 1996].

André Brook Lawn

The estate of E. J. Peters was known by this name in 1871. It was located in the southern portion of Patriots Park, or along Broadway opposite an estate known as Brookside. André Brook passed to the north of André Brook Lawn.
REF: M56.

André's Tree

This was an ancient, enormous tulip tree which towered over the

Major John André
Self-portrait drawn before his execution.
From Lossing's *The Hudson River*.

Post Road until 1801. According to James K. Paulding, it stood "About half a quarter of a mile south of Clark's Kill bridge [the bridge at André Brook], on the high-road...." In other words, it stood along the Post Road where Broadway passes Warner Library today.

The American Citizen newspaper of August 25, 1801, reported that the tree was destroyed by lightning on Saturday, July 21, 1801. It measured 29 feet around at the base, 111 feet in height, 106 feet in diameter at the crown. Some local folk preserved pieces of the tree as keepsakes. The newspaper also recorded that the lightening strike was said to have occurred on the day that news of Benedict Arnold's death in England arrived at Tarrytown.

Letters about the Hudson River and its Vicinity Written in 1835-1837 [AN] relates, in 1837, that the great white-wood was "struck by lightning the very day the news of Gen. Arnold's death was received at Tarrytown." This source gives the circumference of the tree as twenty-six feet, the height [of the trunk?] as forty-one feet.

As the name suggests, the tree is associated with the capture of Major John André, and, indeed, there is a tradition that André was either stopped or searched directly under the tree. However, the actual capture site was certainly closer to the intersection of André Brook and the Post Road, approximately two hundred yards to the north. [See André Brook.] On another score, General Jacob Odell (cited in Bolton [BOL]) recalled that the tree served as an enlistment station for patriots of the vicinity during the spring of 1776. The tree is also associated with several spurious traditions, among them:
- that André was hanged at the tree
- that the tree was destroyed upon receipt of the news of André's death in Tappan
- that the tree stood along André Brook.

Bacon [BA] recounts a legend that, on certain nights, the hoof beats of André's horse could be heard approaching the tree from the north. The name, "Major André's tree," appears in "The Legend of Sleepy Hollow" (1819). Irving almost certainly described the tree from first-hand observations made roughly twenty years earlier. It is not clear when the tree was first given the name, André's Tree, but the name appears to have originated years after the destruction of the tree itself. A remarkable feature of the tree is that it stood, literally, in the middle of the road. That is, the road split to either side of the tree, a unique circumstance.

The narrator of the "Legend of Sleepy Hollow" [IR], describes the neighborhood of the tree in these terms:

> Many dismal tales were told about funeral trains, and mourning cries and wailings heard and seen about the great tree where the unfortunate André was taken. [IR:41]

Later we are told that:

> In the centre of the road stood a gigantic tulip-tree, which towered like a giant above all the trees of the neighborhood, and formed a kind of landmark. Its limbs were gnarled, and fantastic, large enough to form trunks for ordinary trees, twisting down almost to the earth, and rising again into the air. It was connected with the story of the unfortunate André, who had been taken prisoner hard by; and was universally known by the name of Major André's tree. The common people regarded it with a mixture of respect and superstition, and partly from the tales of strange sights and doleful lamentations told concerning it. [IR:44]

When he was writing these words, Irving may have been unaware that the tree had been destroyed by lightning nearly twenty years earlier. If he was accurately describing the tree from his own youthful observations of the landmark, André's Tree had been the target of earlier lightning strikes:

> As he approached a little nearer, he thought he saw something white, hanging in the midst of the tree—he paused and ceased whistling, but on looking more narrowly, he perceived that it was a place where the tree had been scathed by lightning, and the white wood laid bare. [IR:44]

Lossing [LOS:185] refers to the tree as "the stately whitewood." In 1845, Samuel Lyon [MA:172] recalled that he was in a party chasing "Cowboys" (Westchester Loyalist troops) on September 4, 1781, when he observed the enemy troopers, "near André's great white wood tree." Lyon had seen them from the hill above the Old Dutch Church, but the "Cowboys" slipped away before he and his comrades could attack them.

According to a note in Abbott [ABB], the tree was a "...Liriodendron [tulip tree]. It was 112 feet high and stood a noted landmark until, July 31, 1801, when destroyed by lightning. A coincidence was that on the same day the news reached Tarrytown of Arnold's death in London."
See André Brook, Captors' Monument.

VAR: Major André's Tree, Major André's tree, Andre Tree, André tree, the tulip tree; André's great white wood tree.

REF: ABB:28; AN:32-33; BO:229; BOL:volI,321; CON:30; HI:19; IN:57; IR:41,44; LOS:185-186[pic]; M33[COL:129]; M55; MA:172; OW:20; PA:113; SA:354; SC:205; YE:np.

Ardmore

In the late nineteenth century, Ardmore was the summer home of Robert Sewell, a lawyer. It was situated along the south side of Prospect Avenue, just uphill from what is today the Hitachi campus.

REF: M40; SC:245.

Axe Castle

Investment advisors, Emerson W. (d. 1965) and Ruth Houghton Axe (d. 1967), bought this castle and sixty-four acres for $40,000 in 1941. For many years after that time it housed the research department of E. W. Axe & Co. The building was put up for sale by the parent company of Axe Houghton Securities, the company which vacated it in 1992. The investment company would traditionally display an illuminated Christmas star from the battlements during the holiday season. Originally this place was part of the sixty-four-acre estate of General Howard Carroll. *The Tarrytown Centennial Album* [TARR] refers in passing to the structure as Tarrytown Castle. [See Carrollcliff.]

After Mrs. Axe's death in 1967, forty acres on the south side of the castle were sold to the developers of Carrollwood. When Axe Houghton ceased operations here in 1992, the parent company, USF&G, made plans to sell the property. The castle and the remaining acreage were sold in 1994 for $1.9 million. In June of 1994, the *Tarrytown Daily News* [DA] announced that the castle and ten surrounding acres had been sold [March 1994] to a group of investors, 400 Benedict Ave. Corp.

In 1996 renovations were completed on the Castle at Tarrytown,

and the business was opened to the public.
See Carrollwood, Carrollcliff, Barron Court.
REF: CA:230,232; CAST:np; DA[June 17, 1994—also pic]; GE:23; NE [Aug. 21 1994]; ST; TAR:6; TARR:np; TN [May 31 1996 & pic].

Bald Hill

This was apparently a name for Kykuit dating from Revolutionary times. Bald Hill is not an unusual name for high hills, due to the characteristic smooth outcroppings of rock ledge near the top of many hills. See letter in Raymond [RAY].
REF: RAY:13.

Ball Lot

See Jackson's Lot.
REF: MO:17.

Barnhart Park

This is a park off Beekman Avenue in the Village of Sleepy Hollow. It is named for the Reverend John W. Barnhart. This minister was a village resident until his death in 1897. The park is located at the northern end of Barnhart Avenue and to the east of the General Motors plant. Here, Barnhart owned several acres of land.

According to a 1994 village brochure [NO], the park offers "two tennis courts, a basketball court, two volleyball courts, numerous benches and a new children's playground."

Barnhart Park was built on the site of Bay View, the home of Howard H. Morse. See Bay View.
REF CA:201; GE:48; HU:155; M40; M45; NO:np; NOR:np; TAR:44.

Barron Court

Formerly, the estate of Dr. John C. Barron, Barron Court was located north of Tarrytown Road (Route 119) at its intersection with Meadow Street. A twentieth century development, Sleepy Hollow Gardens, is located on this land. The estate had been previously a portion of the lands belonging to Henry Sheldon. It was then owned by J. H. Benedict. (See Sheldon Brook.)

Barron was interested in horticulture. His estate was later purchased by Emil Berolzheimer, a successful manufacturer of pencils. Later, a portion of the Barron property was bought by General

Battle Hill Monument
With Revolutionary War lunette on left.
Photo by Henry Steiner.

Howard Carroll whose estate was known as Carrollcliff.
See Carrollcliff and Maple Terrace.
REF: CA:230,237; M40; SC:246 (pic opp.).

Basher Field

Basher Field was named for the late Thomas Basher, a popular trustee of the Village of Tarrytown. The recreational field includes two ball fields at Losee Park and was dedicated on July 4, 1978.

Thomas Basher was born in Sharon, Pennsylvania, on January 16, 1918; he died in October 1973. Basher moved to Tarrytown in 1953 and was engaged as a district sales manager for a flooring manufacturing company. His tenure as a Tarrytown trustee began in April of 1959 and continued until his death. Throughout this period he served as recreation and fire commissioner. Basher's wife, Emily, succeeded him as a village trustee from 1974 through the April of 1979; his son, Thomas Basher, is currently a village trustee in Tarrytown.

See Losee Park.
REF: BAS; GE:48.

Battle Hill

The hill above the Old Dutch Church of Sleepy Hollow is known by the name of Battle Hill. It is topped by the remains of a Revolutionary War redoubt or, more properly, a lunette. This lunette commanded the Post Road crossing of the Pocantico River in Revolutionary War times. In 1894, a monument was dedicated to the local soldiers of the Revolution on the site.

During the Revolution, on at least one occasion, cattle from the district were driven to safety north of the Pocantico during a British raid, possibly to place them under the protection of the fortified hill. On that day, May 26, 1779, the Refugees (Loyalist militia) attacked the hamlet of Tarrytown and its surroundings. A body of American soldiers, led by a Captain Buchanan, waited in ambush. The Refugees, however, did not advance past the Pocantico. This appears to have been a different incident from the one alluded to in MacDonald [MA:172], when an American contingent at Battle Hill determined to attack a Refugee force near André's Tree. At that time the Refugees moved off to the south, and no engagement ensued.

Ingersoll [IN] writes that this "fortification" dates from 1779,

but that it was never attacked.
> See Jones Hill.
VAR: *Battery Hill [M17]*.
REF *AC:35; CA:42; HU:32; IN:55; JE:384; M17; M42; MA:850-851,172; MI:9-10.; RA:12,13,36; SC:199; TA:map*.

Bay View

The four-acre estate belonging to Howard H. Morse (1842-1911) on Barnhart Avenue (where Barnhart Park lies today) was formerly known by this name. It appears that Morse purchased the house and land from the Titler estate. [See M18].

Bay View overlooked the mouth of the Pocantico River which formed a bay or harbor where it entered the Hudson. [See *Slapershaven*]. The Pocantico was subsequently redirected, the bay was filled in, and the newly created site was used for industrial purposes—ultimately the General Motors Plant and parking lot. See M54 [1855] for a clear representation of the bay-shaped Pocantico River mouth before twentieth century changes.

Morse was an attorney who served as North Tarrytown (Sleepy Hollow) village president for two years. He was also the father of Winfield L. Morse, after whom Morse School is named. The 1912 *New York Times* obituary of Howard H. Morse records that he was born in Rhinebeck, New York, in 1842. He was the author of a work titled "Historic Old Rhinebeck." Morse also practiced law in New York City, and his friends included Samuel J. Tilden, John D. Rockefeller, Sr., and William Rockefeller. His home in North Tarrytown (Sleepy Hollow) is said to have been a summer residence. In the late 1890s, he briefly published a weekly newspaper named *The Sleepy Hollow Mirror*. [See pictures of Morse and his house in HU:156.]

Morse's son, Winfield L. Morse, was also an attorney. A 1959 *New York Times* obituary records that he resided at 7 Millard Avenue at the time of his death. He was for many years (1913-1927) a member of the North Tarrytown (Sleepy Hollow) Board of Education. He later served as counsel to this board, and afterwards, to the consolidated school board of North Tarrytown (Sleepy Hollow) and Tarrytown.

> See also Barnhart Park.

REF: *CA:97,209; DA2 [Sept. 28 1932], [Apr. 16 1942]; HU:155,156*

[pic]; M18; M54; NE [Jan. 3 1912 13:5], [June 23 1959 33:2].

Beaver Hill*

Though not technically in the two villages, Beaver Hill is a significant neighboring topographic feature. It might be considered an eastern limit of the greater Tarrytown area. The hill stands north of Route 119, west of the Saw Mill Parkway and east of Glenville. According to Raymond [RA], American Revolutionary militia forces established a picket station, or guard post, at Farcus Hott on Beaver Hill.

However, Beaver Hill may be an instance of a translocating place name. A map of the Revolutionary period, compiled by Robert Erskine [M66], shows Beaver Hill to lie north of today's Taxter Road and south of Tarrytown Road, on the west side of the Saw Mill River.

See Farcus Hott.

VAR: Beaver Mountain, Beaver's Hill.
REF: M66; M67; RA:112,163; M19; WES:Vol.32, No. 4.

Beekman Farm, the

The name, Beekman Farm, referred to a forty-five acre portion of Cornelia Beekman's (d.1847) extensive holdings, when the parcel was advertised for development. Cornelia was the widow of Gerard Beekman (d. 1822), who purchased the land from the New York State Commissioners of Forfeiture after the Revolution. It is possible that the place name is as old as the Beekman tenure, which began in 1785. The farm extended from André Brook in the south to where the old Croton Aqueduct crosses Broadway at Archville.

The earliest record of the name appears to be that in the *Westchester Record* of December 1822 (cited in Bacon*). Later, when most of Mrs. Beekman's holdings were put up for sale in 1848, the name applied to all of the Beekman Farm [M34].

The original Beekman purchase was 750 acres in extent and cost 9,040 pounds. (New York pounds were about two-thirds the value of pounds sterling.)

Ironically, both the first American ancestor of Gerard Beekman and Frederick Philipse I are said to have arrived in the New World on the same ship with the Dutch Governor Stuyvesant in 1647. Also, Mrs. Cornelia Beekman was a great-grandniece of Frederick Philipse I. [Note: For a list of the purchasers of Philipsburgh from the

Commissioners of Forfeiture, see BOL:vol.II,599.]
   * This advertisement in the *Westchester Record* reads, "*For Sale*. Forty-five acres of very valuable land...." Bacon misinterprets this source. He assumes that the entire farm was offered for sale at this time, and corrects his source to read 450 acres instead of forty-five acres. He appears to compound his error by deducing that large portions of the original purchase had been sold off by this time, which was not the case.
   See Beekmantown.
REF: BA:137; BOL:vol.II,599; HA:71-72; HU:58; M34; PE1: vol.24/3 328; PHIL1:40-41; SC:285; SH:530.

Beekman Forest
   Several hundred acres of woodland belonging to the Gerard G. Beekman estate were known by this name. The forest extended north from the lower Pocantico River and east from the Hudson River to the northeast corner of today's Sleepy Hollow village line. Prior to Beekman's ownership of this tract, the forest was part of the Manor of Philipsburgh. In 1761 Frederick Philipse III leased this land and the rest of the Upper Mills establishment to William Pugsley, with a restriction on the cutting of trees.
   It is not clear when the name "Beekman Forest" originated. Bolton's 1848 history refers to the name. According to a traveler [AN] writing in 1835, "...Beekman woods, [is] the largest forest in Westchester county, and adjacent to the old Dutch Church...."
   See the Mill Woods.
VAR: the Beekman forest, Beekman forest, the Beeckman wood, Beekman's Woods.
REF: AN:56-57; BO:347; BOL:vol.I,546; CA:200; HI:25; HIN:277; HU:24; LE:16; M2; MO:24.

Beekman Grove
   This was a picnic spot of the 1880s located at the foot of Howard Street, off Andrews Lane. As with much of the Village of Sleepy Hollow, it was part of the original Beekman purchase. In 1848 the land, which was to become known as Beekman Grove, belonged to the Stephen D. Beekman estate. Whether it had already acquired the name by that time is not clear. Beekman was the son of Gerard and Cornelia Beekman. [See M34].

A map [M18], reprinted by the Historical Society of the Tarrytowns from Bromley's Atlas of 1881, shows Beekman Grove as the property of Gertrude Beekman. The place stood at the west end of Howard Street, which then ended on a line equal with Pleasant Street.
REF: CA:129; HU:124,131,158; M18; M34.

Beekman Mills, the

The milling establishment near the Beekman mansion (Philipse Castle) was known by this name as late as the 1860s. It was then part of the Ambrose Kingsland estate. This place is the historical restoration called Philipsburg, now operated by Historic Hudson Valley. In the eighteenth century it was often referred to as the Upper Mills.

See the Upper Mills, Philipsburg Manor—Upper Mills.
REF: HA:75.

Beekman Point

Kingsland Point was formerly known by this name. At one time the point was defined by the historic mouth of the Pocantico River. Because the river was redirected and the Pocantico's bay was filled in, the point no longer looks like a point. The river now enters the Hudson several hundred yards to the north of the point, just south of the Kingsland Point Park entrance. The tip of the point is, however, marked by Kidd's Rock, which can be found on the sea wall about two hundred yards north of the Tarrytown Lighthouse. The point was, for a time, named for the Beekmans who owned the surrounding lands from post-Revolutionary times until about 1850. After Gerard Beekman purchased the Upper Mills from the New York State Commissioners of Forfeiture, the point (formerly called "Pugsley's Point") became known as "Beekman Point."

An early map of Mount Pleasant, made by William Adams during the Beekman tenure (about 1797), names the promontory Mill Point.

See Beekman Pond, Kingsland Point, Pugsley's Point, Mill Point.
VAR: Beekman's Point; Beekman's or Kingsland Point.
REF: LE:16; M32; MC:850-851; SC:309.

Beekman Pond

A map in Hutchinson [HU] shows that the mill pond at the Upper Mills (Philipsburg Manor) was know by this name in 1874. Although written examples of the name do not abound, it could be much older. Lederer inaccurately designates the pond as part of Kingsland Point Park. It never was part of the park, although, it was for a time part of the Kingsland estate. This pond was the subject of several nineteenth century bucolic paintings. [See P4 and HO.]

See Mill Pond.

REF: HO:[Pl. 14 & 18]; LE:16; M28; P4.

Beekman Square

This is the triangular island at the intersection of Beekman Avenue and Route 9, near the Sleepy Hollow village hall. Cornelia Beekman donated the plot for "the public use forever" in 1839.

REF: HU:116.

Beekman Suburb, the

By 1848, this name was commonly applied to Beekmantown. Beekmantown was actually considered the suburb of Tarrytown in the mid-nineteenth century.

See the reference in Shonnard. See Beekmantown.

VAR: Pocantico Suburb.
REF: BO:327; BOL:vol.I,531; HU:58; SH:591.

Beekman's Bridge

See Sleepy Hollow Bridge.
REF: RA:196.

Beekman's Landing

This was a Hudson River landing at the foot of the "Road to Landing," as it is named in the Adams map (about 1797). The road was the precursor of Beekman Avenue.
REF: M32.

Beekmantown

This name has been incorrectly considered an early name for the Village of Sleepy Hollow. Strictly speaking, Sleepy Hollow is a modern incorporated village; Beekmantown was not incorporated and the name applied to a much smaller area. E. M. Bacon, a local historian writing in the 1890s, records that the name originally applied to a triangular area between Beekman Avenue, Cortlandt Street, and the Hudson. Apparently, Beekmantown started with these dimensions, but a few years later it appears to have included most of land between André Brook and Beekman Avenue.

An early incidence of the name occurs in an advertisement of 1835, in which Cornelia Beekman (d. 1847) offered a portion of her land for sale. The name appears again in the map accompanying the 1848 edition of Bolton.

According to Bacon, the name continued in use for at least twenty-five years after the incorporation of North Tarrytown in 1874. The mid-nineteenth century *Gazetteer of the State of New York* by J. H. French (cited in Shonnard) refers to Beekmantown as, " a suburb of Tarrytown."

See Beekman Farm.

VAR: *Beekman Town, Beeckmantown, Beekmanville.*
REF: *BA:139; BOL:vol.I,531,549; CA:148; CON:28; GE:11; HU:2,52,58,72; LE:16; M51; M52; M57; SC:287; SH:591; TAR:2,4; TR:np.*

Beekman Town Landing

This landing appears on a map of 1848. It was located just south of the foot of Beekman Street (Beekman Avenue). Twenty years later, in M38, the name appears to have fallen from use, and the feature is shown as the dock at Husted's Yard.

See Beekman's Landing.
REF: *M34; M38.*

Benedict Estate, the

In the mid-nineteenth century this was the four hundred-acre estate of General James Benedict. Benedict's daughter, Ann, was married to Captain Edward Cobb. [See also Cobb's Lot.] The Benedict estate extended from the Hudson River to the Saw Mill River, including the ground between White Plains Road (Route 119) and the Tarrytown Lakes.

A passing reference in Canning [CA] yields the twentieth century name for this extensive early nineteenth century tract. A recently published book, *Images of America Tarrytown and Sleepy Hollow*, indicates that Rosehill was the name of General Benedict's mansion; it was perhaps the name of his estate. The land on which Washington Irving School stands was once known as the Benedict-Cobb property.

Earlier, the land was owned by Captain George Comb (d.1827) and Colonel James Hammond (d.1810). These two local Revolutionary War veterans had purchased the land at the sale of Philipse Manor after the Revolution. Prior to the war, this land was the tenant farm of Comb's father-in-law, Thomas Wildey, who was said to have been killed in the Battle of White Plains. Wildey paid an annual rent of twelve pounds, nine shillings. According to *The Old Dutch Burying Ground of Sleepy Hollow* [HIS], Thomas Wildey's farm included 262 acres.

Comb and Hammond sold the farm to Ralph Van Houter in 1790. According to Scharf [SC], early in the nineteenth century, it was owned by an Englishman named Cumberford who experimented in the raising of sheep. Then in 1826 the farm was sold by a man named Barnardus Swartout to General James Benedict.

VAR: the Benedict farm, the Benedict-Cobb property.
REF: CA:203-204,232; HIS:41; M42; SC:232.

Benedict Park

According to Canning [CA], this is a 1924 residential development on twenty-six acres of land formerly known as Cobb's Lot. It was developed by Samuel E. and John Miller. The development was named for the Benedict family, who had extensive real estate holdings in the area.

See also Benedict estate. See Miller Park.

REF: CA:163,204; DA(Buxton's letter of late 1981); DA2 [Oct. 9 1934]; TAR:40.

Biseghtick Creek

This was the Delaware Indian name for Sunnyside Brook. The brook runs along the Irvington-Tarrytown border and was named in the Royal Charter for Philipsburgh of 1693.

See Sunnyside Brook.

VAR: Bisightick, Bissightick.
REF: BOL:vol.I,268; BOL:vol.II,592; TA:9; WES:Vol.12,No.4,p.85.

Boxwood
This was an early name for the John D. Rockefeller estate, Kykuit, as found on a map of 1926.
See Kaakoote, Kykuit.
REF: M29.

Braemar
This name applied to the twenty-four-acre estate of G. B. Newton, which stood on the north side of Tarrytown Road, east of the Croton Aqueduct, and west of Barron Court. Newton owned the place during the late 1800s; he subsequently sold the estate to Judge Rumsey Miller about 1904.
Prior to Newton's tenure a large stone house had been built about 1850 by William H. Townsend. Townsend sold the property to Lewis Roberts.
See the Luke Estate.
REF: CA:236; M40.

Breastworks Lot, the
This is the name of a parcel on Kykuit Hill, formed by the intersection of Bedford Road and County House Road. According to M. D. Raymond, a local historian who wrote in 1890, military earthworks were constructed on this land in 1776, when General George Washington made the Davids' farmhouse a temporary headquarters. Bacon, too, tells the story that General Washington stopped at the Davids Homestead after the Battle of White Plains. It was said that a party of English soldiers arrived shortly after Washington's departure and slashed at the doorposts of the farm house in frustration.
Raymond adds that the place was "long known" by this name.
REF: RAY:12; WES:Vol.32, No. 4.

Brick Yard Row
This short row of houses stood near the west end of Beekman Avenue in the nineteenth century. Scharf [SC] wrote that in 1850 a Catholic priest from St. John's College, Fordham, held religious services in a small room at Mrs. Cain's home.
Brick Yard Row was a street near the Brick Yard of Mr. Wood. In 1885 Wood sold his property to the Rand Drill Works, a

manufacturer of steam and compressed air powered rock drills used in blasting. [See GM.]

Brick Yard Row could have been today's Hudson Street, or possibly a short section of Beekman Avenue facing the brickyard. However, a Tarrytown Daily News article of 1933 asserts that Brick Yard Row was a street running west from Cortlandt Street.

See Hunk Alley.

VAR: Brick-Yard Row.
REF: DA2 [Oct. 13 1933]; GM:8; HU:72; M18; M38; SC;300.

Briggsville

Briggsville is a residential area at the intersection of Sleepy Hollow Road and Bedford Road. The land was formerly owned by Amos Briggs, who came to the Tarrytowns in 1836. His brother John had a meat market on Main Street.

REF: CA:201; CAL1; HU:182,235.

Broadway

See Albany Post Road.

Brookside

This was the estate of E. J. Blake, which stood east of Broadway. The estate was divided by André Brook.

REF: M18; M38; M56.

Brookside Park

The area of Patriots Park was, in the early twentieth century, known by this name. In Revolutionary times, the area was known as Wiley's Swamp. André Brook runs through the park.

See Patriots Park, André Brook and Wildey's Swamp.

REF: HU:147,227.

Brown's Pond

This is (or was) a pond in Pennybridge, located near Sheldon Avenue. It seems to have had some connection with Clarence Brown's ice houses on Sheldon Avenue.

REF: CA:129,239; DA [Sept. 15 1914, p.1].

Buckley Estate

A 1932 book, *Tarrytown and the Tarrytown National Bank*, shows this estate to have been located on the west side of Broadway, just south of the St. Vincent de Paul School and north of the Luke Estate. This was formerly part of the Hoe estate, Maplehurst. Prior to that it was part of the post-Revolutionary William Hunt farm.

See Maplehurst.
REF: DA2 [Aug. 5 1942]; TA:map.

Burnt House, the*

See Youngs Corners.
VAR: *Youngs' Burnt House.*
REF: SC:312; SH:461.

Buttermilk Hill*

Buttermilk Hill is a long ridge running north/south along the western bank of the Saw Mill River. The southern end of Buttermilk Hill slopes down to the northern end of the Tarrytown Lakes. On the eastern side of the hill lies the Saw Mill River and the old Putnam Railroad bed—now a bike trail. On the hill's western side is the hamlet of Pocantico Hills. Buttermilk Hill does not lie within the borders of Sleepy Hollow and Tarrytown, but it does have a strong historic connection with the two villages. A reference to Buttermilk Hill quoted in Raymond [RA] predates 1820, and it seems probable that the name is at least as old as Revolutionary times.

A picturesque story of the name's derivation is to be found in Owens [OW]. It is said that in the time of the Revolution, cows were herded to this out-of-the-way location for safekeeping from the thieving "Cowboys" and "Skinners." These were local outlaw bands which ravaged the "Neutral Ground." Local residents would go to the hill to milk their cows and bring home butter and milk.

Bacon relates that at the time of the 1863 New York City draft riots many local African-Americans fled for safety to Buttermilk Hill. They felt threatened by the mob sweeping north along the Post Road toward the Tarrytown area.

VAR: *Mont Buttermilk*
REF: BA:85,145; CON:33; DA2 [May 24 1937]; M15; M66; M67; OW:[map],21,30; RA:60,68. RAYM:np; SC:305; TA:37; TARR:np; WES:Vol.32, No. 4; YE:np.

Captors' Monument, the

This monument, located on a plot of ground between Patriots Park and Broadway, is dedicated to the three local militiamen who captured Major John André on September 22, 1780. Yet common usage often associates it with their British prisoner.

An earlier monument was erected on the site in 1853, but it was improved in 1880 and surmounted with a bronze statue by a sculptor named William Rudolph O'Donovan (b. 1844). O'Donovan, a self-taught sculptor who served in the Confederate Army, enjoyed great popularity in New York during the late nineteenth century. On the eastern side of the base is a bronze relief of the capture sculpted by Theodore Bauer.

The statue is said to depict John Paulding, the leading spirit of the three captors. Late in life John Romer, a contemporary witness to the events, recalled that "John Paulding was a bold and enterprising man...." Romer went on to describe how Paulding was one day with a militia contingent on Kykuit Hill when a party of Refugees (American Loyalists) was observed near Tarrytown. When Paulding's comrades refused to attack the superior force, he attacked them single-handedly, firing his musket several times from cover and escaping into the bushes. In another episode, again on "Davis's Hill" (Kykuit), Paulding urged a band of fifteen or twenty militia to attack a Yager contingent at Tarrytown. After the attack, Paulding was the last to retreat, making his way through rocks and swamp. On other occasions Paulding's daring led to his capture. In fact he had made a remarkable escape from prison in New York City only four days before he participated in the capture of André. The Hessian coat which Paulding had been given in prison, and which he wore at the time of the capture, may have led André to accidentally betray himself.

Before the monument was established, many visitors to the area (including President Martin Van Buren) would lament that no memorial had been set up to commemorate the capture of André. [See AN.] The land for the monument was donated by an African-American couple of the nineteenth century, Mr. and Mrs. William Taylor. The Taylors were former slaves from Virginia. They moved to Tarrytown from New York City in 1850 and lived west of Broadway between André Brook and Wildey Street. [See also André Brook and André's Tree.] The story goes that the Taylors lived comfortably and were public minded citizens, but they died poor after

Captors' Monument
Bas relief on base depicting the capture of Major André. Photo by Henry Steiner.

being cheated by an unscrupulous real estate agent. Mr. Taylor died in 1880 and was buried at Sleepy Hollow Cemetery. See TARR for pictures of Mrs. Taylor and her great-great-granddaughter, Mrs. Richard Plater, *nee* Marie Jackson.

See Patriots Park, André Brook and André's Tree

VAR: *The André Monument, André's Monument, André's Captors' Monument, André Capture Monument; Captors' monument, the André monument, André's Monument, André Monument at Tarrytown.*

REF: AN:32; BOL:vol.I,346; BACO:7; CH:[No. 18 June 1990,np]; DA2 [Sept. 29 1930]; HAD2:60; HAND:22 [pic],25; HUFE:3-7,82; HUT:47-51; LO:330-331; M3; M18; M29; M42; MI:1; MO:8[pic],9; OW:20: RAYM:np; SA:354,356; SH:471; ST; TAP:np; TARR:np [& pic]; TN [Aug. 16 1996]; WES:Vol.6:113; YE:np.

Carl Brook, the

A tributary of the Pocantico, the Carl Brook intersects Sleepy Hollow Road at the northeast village boundary line of Sleepy Hollow. Most of the brook extends into Pocantico Hills. It was said to be a good trout stream in the mid-nineteenth century. Bacon tells of the Reverend Abel T. Stewart, a pastor of the Old Dutch Church (1852-1866), who avidly fished the Carl, the Gedney, and the Pocantico.

The brook appears to have been named for the same "Carl" as that of Carl's Mill.

Sources for this place name include Edgar Mayhew Bacon [BA], and three maps: the plan of the Tarrytown Heights Land Company [M36], the Map of North Tarrytown 1877 [M65], and the 1867 Beers map [M35]. Another map of 1891 [M40] shows Carlsbrook Road running parallel to this stream.

See Carl's Mill.

VAR: *Carls Brook, Carles Brook.*
REF: BA:60; M35; M36; M40; M41; M65; Pl.

Carl Estate

This is land which belonged to Thomas Carl, who in 1871 owned lands adjoining the holdings of the Tarrytown Land Company. [See M36.] The estate extended east of the Pocantico River and south of the Carl Brook.

See the Carl Brook and Carl's Mill.

REF: M36; M40.

Carl's Mill*
   A map [M35] shows the site of Carl's Mill to be just outside the present day northeast border of the Village of Sleepy Hollow. However, the Carl Brook intersects the Pocantico within the village boundaries. Note, Dorland's map [M57] is not reliable for the location of the mill, which shows it where Lister's Mill should be.
   According to Bacon [BA], Carl's Mill was previously known as Hart's Mill. Bacon seems mistaken on this point; Hart's Mill was on the Pocantico, Carl's Mill was on a tributary, the Carl Brook. [See M35.]   Each mill had its own pond.   According to Hutchinson [HU:22], Hart's Mill may have at one time been a Philipse mill.
   Bacon adds that Carl's Mill was a sawmill establishment frequented by Washington Irving.   Indeed, Irving was a visitor to Carl's Mill, but the mill was a grist mill, not a saw mill; Hart's Mill may have been a saw mill. Two works of Irving's describe Carl's Mill as a grist mill. Here is the reference in "Wolfert's Roost":

> In a remote part of the hollow where the Pocantico forced its way down rugged rocks, stood Carl's Mill, the haunted house of the neighborhood....an old Negro thrust his head all dabbled with flour out of a hole above the waterwheel.... [IR:311]

   A similar passage in " Sleepy Hollow," which does not mention Carl's Mill by name, reads:

> ...an old goblin-looking mill, situated among rocks and water-falls, with clanking wheels and rushing streams, and all kinds of uncouth noises....an old negro thrust out his head, all dabbled with flour.... [IRVING]

   Irving goes on to write, in both works, that this African-American millhand was a primary source for the story of the Headless Horseman.
   A drawing of Carl's Mill appeared in *Gleason's Pictorial*, June 11, 1853, showing the mill in a derelict, but picturesque condition.
   See Sleepy Hollow Mill, the Carl Brook, Carl Estate, Hart's Mill.
VAR: *Carve's Mill, Carl's mill.*

Carl's Mill
As it appeared in *Gleason's Pictorial* on June 11, 1853.

Castle Philipse
Now restored at Philipsburg Manor—
Upper Mills. Etching by Lossing.

REF: BA:140; BAC:239; HARP:np[pic]; HU:48[pic]; IR:311; IRVING:9; M35; M57; P1[caption & article].

Carrollcliff

This was the estate owned by the family of General Howard Carroll (1854-1916) from 1900 to 1941. Carroll had the castle built in the first decade of the twentieth century. The castle has been known for the last few decades as Axe Castle, and it was owned for a long time by Axe-Houghton Securities. Most of this land has now been developed as condominiums. The neo-Gothic castle still stands and is today a hotel and restaurant named "The Castle at Tarrytown." The estate and castle served as a backdrop for several motion pictures.

Carrollcliff's sixty-four acres were formed by lands purchased from Dr. John Barron and William H. Webb. General Carroll owned a steamship line, the Glen Island Amusement Park, and a paving company. He was also a successful playwright and the president of the New York Hudson-Fulton Tercentenary in 1909. He received his appointment to the rank of brigadier general from a New York governor. Carroll's father had been a Union general who died at the Civil War Battle of Antietam.

See Axe Castle, Barron Court and Carrollwood.
VAR: Carrollcliffe.
REF: CA:230-232; CAST:np; CON:23,35; DI; NE [Aug. 21 1994]; ST; TA:map; TN [May 31 1996 & pic]; ZU:89.

Carrollwood

This is a development of twelve condominium complexes (a total of 208 units) built on forty acres of land formerly part of Carrollcliff.

See Axe Castle and Carrollcliff.
REF: NE [Aug. 21 1994]; TN [May 31 1996 & pic].

Castle, The

See Castle Ridge.
VAR: the Castle.
REF: MI:219.

Castle Philipse

Castle Philipse is a name for the manor house at the Upper Mills, now known as Philipsburg Manor Restoration. The name, Castle Philipse, dates back to at least the mid-nineteenth century.

Adolphus Philipse doubled the size of his father's original manor house when he ordered a stone addition in 1720. After the Revolution, the Beekmans made a large wood-frame addition, and in the late nineteenth century Ambrose Kingsland made further modifications. Elsie Janis, an actress, owned the manor house from 1916-1937. For a short time afterwards the Castle was home to the Historical Society of the Tarrytowns. Then John D. Rockefeller, Jr., was instrumental in having the property conveyed to Sleepy Hollow Restorations, now known as Historic Hudson Valley. In the 1960s the manor house was excavated and rebuilt along with the mill and dam. The restoration recreates the dwelling in the period of Adolphus's mid-eighteenth century tenure.

It seems that Washington Irving never wrote about Castle Philipse and its mill. But the description of the Baltus Van Tassel farm in "The Legend of Sleepy Hollow" might well have been based on "the Castle" in the post-Revolutionary days of the Beekman ownership.

See Philipse Castle.

VAR: *Philipse-his-castle, Flypse's Castle, Castle Philipse, castle Philipse, Philipse' Castle, Philipse Castle, Philipse Castle Restoration, Castle Phillipse [sic.—IN], Castle Phillips [sic.—P4]the Castle [Lossing, PE1], Fylipsen Castle, Flypse his Castle; the Castle; PHILI:41-54; OE:18.*

REF: *BA:ix,5,13; BOL:vol.I,511,531; CON:np.,25-28; CRA:166[& pic]; DA2 [Jan. 25 1943]; DU:4; HA:66; HAR [Apr. 1876, p. 642-643]; HI:21; HIN:272,283; IN:40,56; LO:325-327; M22; M42; M44; M57; MO:6; PE1:vol.24/3 321,323,326-334; P3; P4; PHI:np; PHILI:31,41,47,49-55; SH:255,162-163; TWO:122,134; WI:138.*

Castle Ridge

This name refers to the height on which Marymount College stands today. Canning [CA] seems to consider Castle Ridge part of the Tarrytown Heights district. It was formerly occupied by the B. F. Hermann residence and, in early days, Hackley Lower School was located here. The ridge is named for the castle-like mansion designed by Alexander Jackson Davis which stood below Castle Avenue, today's Marymount Avenue. The mansion was also known as "Herrick's Folly" because it was erected at great expense by John J.

Herrick between 1854 and 1856. Herrick (d. 1887) was an entrepreneur in the steamship business. He occupied the building until 1861, when under pressure from business failures he sold it to a Mr. Dimmock. The castle was subsequently owned by a Englishman named Mitchell (a reputed recluse), and then by William B. Hatch, who in 1873 paid $40,000 for the estate which had once cost $100,000. Hatch took his own life after his business failed. His brother, A. S. Hatch, was the next owner of the estate, living there with his family for many years. He served as president of the New York Stock Exchange, and he was one of the organizers of the Putnam railroad line.

The place subsequently changed hands several more times. Mrs. Theodore Irving opened her school for ladies, St. John's, there in 1890. It was then purchased by Miss Cassity Eliza Mason, who had been conducting a girls' school named the Eastman School in Philadelphia. According to historian Wally Buxton (WES:Vol.34), Mason relocated her school to Castle Ridge in 1895. Afterwards, it was called the "Castle School" until its close in 1933. Mark Twain was said to have been a guest at Miss Mason's school on several occasions. [See Halleston for more on Mark Twain.] The building was razed in 1944. The Frank D. Cooney, Jr., house on Castle Heights Avenue was built on the Castle's foundation, using much of the old stone.

VAR: the Castle.
REF: AR [Dec. 3 1887]; CA:152,153,209,232,313; CON:35; DA2 [Mar. 12 1937 pic], [Mar. 12 1937]; HISTOR:np; HUFE:84,95; LE:26; M40; M42; MI:21; TARR:np; WES:[Fall 1994, p.78]; WES:Vol.34:15-16; ZU:97 [& pic].

Catfish Pond

This is the very small pond lying on the east side of the Lower Lake. In the late 1950s, the writer and his childhood friends would go there to "get in trouble." Catfish Pond is an interesting place name; it does not appear to be found on any published map, yet the name is commonly used by residents of the two villages, particularly "old-timers." In the 1950s it was a good place to hunt for turtles and frogs, and it still contains sunfish, bass, and carp.

The pond was separated from the rest of the Lower Lake by the railroad bed which hooked around the lakes in the 1880s. Part of this

railroad bed has been converted into a paved recreational trail.
REF: ST.

Cedars, the

The riverside estate of George S. Scott stood between the bottom of Church Street and the Hudson River in the late 1860s. It was owned several years later by a Mr. Schmidt. Afterwards it was owned by Anton Schwarz, who was in the beer business. According to Canning [CA], the mansion, stables, and gatehouse were still standing on lower Church Street in the early 1970s.
REF: CA:235; M38; M56.

Cedar Cliff

The estate of William Earl Dodge (1805-1883) lay to the west of where Transfiguration Church stands today. Dodge gave his name to Phelps-Dodge, a metals company. He was born near Hartford, Connecticut, on September 4, 1805, and was married to the second daughter of Anson Greene Phelps. Dodge was involved in many industries: metals, lumber, insurance, railroads. His wealth at the time of his death in February 1883 was estimated at five million dollars. It was his custom to spend summers at his Tarrytown estate, and in 1882 he entertained former president Rutherford B. Hayes there. In 1880 Dodge served briefly as president of the "Monument Association of the Capture of André."

During Reconstruction, Dodge was a United States Congressman from New York City. He was also a leader of the national temperance movement and a founder of the YMCA. Dodge acquired Cedar Cliff [see M38] from J. G. Dudley by 1868. By 1891, the twelve acres of Cedar Cliff were owned by John Dustin Archbold. [See map in CA.] Archbold (1848-1916) was the man who took over the reins of the Standard Oil Company from John D. Rockefeller, Sr. Archbold's large Romanesque mausoleum in Sleepy Hollow Cemetery stands near the tomb of another Standard Oil partner, William Rockefeller.

REF: AR [Feb. 17 1883]; CA:157,234; DI:Vol.1,p337; DI:Vol.3,352-353; HUFE:85; M29; M38; M40; M56; NE [Aug. 21 1994]; SC:245; TA:31; YE:np.

Cedar Hill

A modern United States Geological survey map uses this name for the hill which stands above Douglas Park. Lederer [LE] describes the hill's location as east of the Pocantico River, near the end of High Street.

See Prospect Hill and Jones Hill.

REF: LE:27,73; M19.

Cedar Lawn

A mansion was built on this estate in 1847. [The writer has no information on the estate's location.] The property was purchased about 1880 by Isaac Stern, president of a New York dry goods firm, and the mansion became known in the twentieth century as the "Isaac Stern Castle." See Wally Buxton's article in *The Westchester Historian* [WES] for more information about Cedar Lawn.

REF: WES:Vol.34:16.

Cemetery Hill

Broadway runs by the Old Dutch Church of Sleepy Hollow on Cemetery Hill. The writer has heard the hill commonly referred to by this name.

REF: HU:116; ST.

Centennial Tower, the

This was a round, stone tower which stood in what is today Philipse Manor. The tower was constructed by order of Ambrose Kingsland in 1875 to commemorate the centennial of American Independence. It was built of local stone extracted from the quarry which once existed near the Philipse Manor Station. Scharf describes the tower as standing "...directly east of the Hudson River Railroad track, on an abrupt rocky height...." Bacon refers to it as "Kingsland's round-tower, at the old quarry." The precise location of the tower is indicated in an 1891 map [M40].

See Quarry Castle. See a picture in Hutchinson [HU].

REF: BA:107; BAC:238[Ill.]; HU:117,118[pics],183; M40; SC:310; TN [Nov. 22 1996], [Apr. 19 1996 pic].

Charter Oak, the

The Charter Oak was a venerable, immense oak tree noted by

Edgar Mayhew Bacon [BA]. It stood on the rise of ground overlooking the Upper Mills from the south. Bacon could not say how the tree got this name, but recalls that during his youth in the 1860s the tree was destroyed by vandals.
REF: BA:122.

Clark's Kill

This brook is better known by its later name, André Brook. Captain John Romer, a Revolutionary War veteran, observed that André Brook was known as Clark's Kill at the time of the Revolution. His statement was borne out by James K. Paulding, writing in the 1820s. Who Clark was, is not clear.

See André Brook.
VAR: Clarks Kill.
REF: ABB:28; HU:35; LE:30; M57; MC:146,281; PA:109; RA:177.

Clark's Kill Bridge

There was obviously a Post Road bridge crossing Clark's Kill in the days before paved highways and culverts. James K. Paulding is the only writer (to our knowledge) to give the bridge a name. In the days of the American Revolution, the highway appears to have crossed the brook about 150 to 200 yards further east of its present location. As noted elsewhere in this work, portions of Broadway were redirected during the building of the old Croton Aqueduct. Today the stream passes, unseen, down the eastern hillside and under Broadway through a culvert. It reemerges in Patriots Park.

See Clark's Kill and André Brook.
REF: PA:113.

Clear View

In the late nineteenth century, the estate of Charles J. Gould had this name. Earlier, it was part of the much larger holding of Jacob Storm. Clear View consisted of seven and a half acres lying north of Mekeel Avenue, east of Woodland Avenue, and west of Beech Lane. In the early 1960s (and before) this land was known as Sun Cliff. To the best of the writer's knowledge, it was a kind of spa or retreat. According to Canning [CA], there was an open air amphitheater on the old estate. In the late 1960s the land was developed with houses.

The Industrial Workers of the World (IWW) held a meeting here in May 1914. They had come to the Tarrytown business district at Orchard Street to protest World War I and working conditions in the Colorado mines controlled by John D. Rockefeller, Sr. Several of the group's leaders were arrested after attempting to speak in the Orchard Street district. This raised freedom-of-speech issues which brought "muckraker" author, Upton Sinclair, to town. The group of protesters was finally granted permission to hold a rally, but no hall was open to them. Mrs. Charles D. Gould offered her estate to help defuse the situation. The meeting took place without further incident.

The IWW returned on June 22, 1914, and staged an unscheduled outdoor rally near the intersection of Mekeel Avenue and the old Croton Aqueduct. This time a riot ensued when local residents began to hurl objects at the protesters. Mounted New York City watershed police were called in to escort the beleaguered demonstrators back to Tarrytown Railroad Station. [See TARR for more.]

See Suncliff, Mount Hope, Wilson Park.

VAR: Clearview.
REF: CA:237; DA2 [March 29 1935]; M18; M40; TARR:np[& pic].

Cobb's Lot

The lot was a twenty-six-acre parcel named for Captain Edward Cobb (d. 1895) and his wife Ann Benedict Cobb. Canning [CA] gives the date of Mrs. Cobb's death as both 1888 and 1891. The former seems to be the more likely date. Captain Cobb had interests in a Liverpool packet line.

Their mansion, formerly the home of Mrs Cobb's father, stood on the site of today's Washington Irving School. According to the late Wally Buxton, a former village historian, the lot stretched "from West Franklin Street to the rear yards of the homes on the north side of Church Street and from Broadway to the railroad tracks near the Hudson River." This would include all of today's Miller Park. In the years between 1897 and 1924, the lot served as an unofficial recreational field. Buxton associates it with football and baseball games, campfires, snowball fights, amateur astronomy, horseback riding, and wild flowers.

REF: CA:42,74,163-164,204; DA [Sept. 2 1981 (also North Tarrytown (Sleepy Hollow) village historian's letter several days later)]; M35; M38; M42; TARR:np.

Cold Spring

Edgar Mayhew Bacon writes that "a prosaic drinking-trough" marked the place where the Cold Spring crossed Broadway. This was before the turn of the twentieth century. The trough was replaced early in the twentieth century by Fremont Fountain. On its run from the cemetery to the Hudson the spring feeds Fremont Pond.

See Fremont Fountain, Cold Spring Fountain, Fremont Spring.
REF: BA:88; M65.

Cold Spring Fountain

The fountain was commissioned by William Rockefeller and dedicated to John C. Frémont. A North Tarrytown stone worker, Giacomo Ceconi (1886-1973), made the structure, which replaced an earlier trough. The fountain still stands on Broadway opposite Peabody Field. The stream which feeds the fountain and Fremont Pond has been known as Cold Spring.

See Fremont Spring, Fremont Fountain, Cold Spring.
VAR: Cold Spring fountain.
REF: AL:153-155; CA:222; CE; HU:86; MO:27.

Columbus Square

This is a later name for Fountain Square. The square, located near the foot of Valley Street, was rededicated on October 12, 1933. Present at the ceremony were members of the St. Elmo Council, the Federation of Italian-American Societies of the Tarrytowns, and the Knights of Columbus. More than 2,000 people attended.

See Fountain Square.
REF:CA:237; DA2 [Oct. 13 1932], [Sept. 10 1937 & pic].

Conklin's*

According to Jenkins [JE], Conklin's was the farm of Jacob Conklin in Tarrytown, one of four overseers of the Post Road in 1742. The road from Kingsbridge to Conklin's measured twenty-two miles in 1779. Conklin was the overseer of that portion of the road extending from Thomas Storm's farm to the Upper Mills.

A modern history of Irvington [WO] reports that Conklin's served as a tavern on the Post Road in what is today the Village of Irvington. From 1746 it was owned by Mathias and Sophia Conklin, having passed into the Conklin family at the death of Jan Harmse in

1742. In 1771 it was recorded as being the second stop on the highway to Albany. In 1774 Jonathan Odell took over the tavern and the surrounding farm.
See Mile 32.
VAR: Cocklins.
REF: JE:344; WO:12-13.

Cooney's Dock
This dock is located on the Tarrytown waterfront at Tarrytown Point, just north of Losee Park.
See Point Landing, Steamboat Landing, Tarrytown Point.
REF: ST; TN [Aug. 2 1996].

County House Road
The County House was the name for the county "poor house" in East View. Part of this road, which runs along the south side of Kykuit, connects Route 448 with the Tarrytown Lakes. It was partially diverted upon the establishment of the Tarrytown Lakes. The road is also referred to as Tower Hill Road.
See Tower Hill, the Lower Cross Road.
VAR: County House Road, the old; County House Road, the.
REF: DA2 [May 24 1937]; M21; SC:205; ST; WES:Vol.32, No. 4.

Creek of Beekman Mills
Surveyor William Adams referred to the Pocantico River by this name about 1797. It seems to apply specifically to that stretch below the Beekman mill.
REF: M32.

Crest Lawn
This was the twenty-acre estate of Bainbridge S. Clark, east of Broadway and south of Tarrytown Road. The place was known for its lawns and fountains.
REF: CA:236; M40.

Croydon
This estate name appears on a map of 1926. It lay in the same place as the old Sheldon estate, near the mouth of Sheldon Brook.
See Sheldon Brook, Millbrook, Old Van Weert Mill.

REF: M29.

Croton Aqueduct, the
To most people in the Tarrytowns, this name generally means the Old Croton Aqueduct. Construction of this engineering marvel began in 1837. John B. Jervis was the engineer who completed the project. The muscle for the job was provided mainly by an Irish immigrant labor force of nearly 4,000; there were two workers' "insurrections" during the period of construction.

Water flowed through the aqueduct for the first time on June 22, 1842, but the project was not complete until 1848. The aqueduct tunnel measured 7' 8" to 8' 5.5" high. After an upgrade the aqueduct carried as much as 95 million gallons per day in the late nineteenth century. By the mid-twentieth century it carried a lower rate of 35 million gallons per day until 1955. It then served only .8 million gallons per day to a single Westchester community until it was decommissioned in September 1965. In 1974 it was listed on the National Register of Historic Places, and in 1976 the state legislature named it a Scenic and Historic Corridor. The aqueduct tunnel is now used as a route for phone and sewage lines. Construction on the New Croton Aqueduct, which travels a different route, began in 1885.

Today the top of the aqueduct serves as a unique recreational trail, suitable for hiking, running and biking. One particularly interesting sight is the large stone structure, or viaduct, which crosses the Pocantico River in Sleepy Hollow Cemetery. There are also various stone ventilators and "waste weirs" at intermittent locations in the Tarrytowns.

Previously, there was an arch where the aqueduct crosses Route 9 at Archville [see TN] which was removed in the 1920s. See a pamphlet concerning the Old Croton Aqueduct [CRO] for a hiking guide to the whole aqueduct.

The Aqueduct is named for the Village of Croton, which is in turn named for an early American Indian chief. According to Lederer [LE], "Croton is an adaptation of the name of a chief, Kentotin or Knoten, who lived near the mouth of the [Croton] river."

The Croton River supplied all of the water transmitted through the aqueduct to New York City. The river empties into the Hudson just south of Croton Point.

See old Croton Aqueduct.

VAR: The Aqueduct, Old croton Aqueduct; Old Croton Aqueduct.
REF: CA:32,47; COR:2; CRO:1-15[& pics.]; ST; HU:55; LE:36; M21; M35; M47; P2; TN [Oct. 31 1996], [Oct. 2 1996 & pics.], [Aug.163 1996], [June 21 1996 & pic], [Nov. 2 1995 & pic]; TR:np; M65TAR:29; WES:Vol.32, No. 4; WES:Vol.34:16.

Cunningham Castle

At the turn of the twentieth century this was an estate near the Jay Gould holdings and the former Bierstadt estate.
REF: IN:51.

Davids' Hill

This was an alternate name for Kykuit—the hill on which the Rockefeller mansion is located. The Davids family owned the land through the Revolutionary period. The Davids house, which is described in Scharf and Bacon, was built in the mid-eighteenth century and is said to have been visited by Washington in the time of the Battle of White Plains. It is also said to be the place where the three captors of Major André parted company from their main party, just before intercepting the British spy.

In colonial times the hillside was farmed by William Davids, Esq. (1707-1787), a tenant of Philipsburgh Manor. Davids was a justice of the peace as well as a town supervisor. During the Revolution he was a member of the Committee of Safety and a soldier. At the time of the Revolution, Davids paid an annual rent (to Frederick Philipse III) of 5 pounds, 14 shillings, and 6 pence. There were two other Davids on Philipsburgh, David and Jacobus, who also appear on the rent rolls.

William Davids' son (baptized 1735) was a private in the militia and a "Westchester Guide." The son was wounded and left for dead during a skirmish at Verplank's Point on July 17, 1779. He survived and was excused from further military service due to his wounds at the recommendation of New York Governor George Clinton.

During the Revolutionary War, John Romer was, for a time, a guide with Colonel Armand's "legion." Romer later recalled that while posted on Davids' Hill, he saw a British frigate send a boat toward Beekman's Point.

In the early 1890s, the hill was part of the John R. Stephens estate, which was purchased by John D. Rockefeller, Sr., in 1893. Stephens' wife was a descendant of the Davids family.

A map [M1] shows the Davids house located on the north side of County House Road at the road's intersection with André Brook. According to Owens [OW], the house was rebuilt in the twentieth century and served as home to Nelson A. Rockefeller, a governor of New York State.

See Hawes in Raymond [RA]. See Kykuit.

VAR: *The Davids' Homestead, Davids homestead, Davis' Hill, Davis's Hill.*

REF: *ABB:28; BA:135; BOL:vol.I,551; CON:37[bot]; EA:[appendix] 106; HIS:50; M1; M6; M12; M17; M28; M37; M42; M55; M57; MC:850-851; NEV:288-289 vol.2; OW:20; RA:172-174, 205; RAY:13; SC:205; SH:471; YE:np; WES:Vol.32, No. 4.*

De Vries Field

This modern recreational field is sometimes called the Marsh Field, possibly because it was built on a marsh and still neighbors one. It may also have inherited the name from the playing field which once stood at the west end of Continental Street, the Marsh (Donohue Field). Sleepy Hollow resident, Walter Ceconi, recalls that De Vries Field was built largely through volunteer labor and donated materials and equipment.

Margaret Hardenbroek De Vries was the widow of Peter De Vries, a wealthy merchant of New Amsterdam. She became the first wife of Frederick Philipse I (the first lord of Philipsburgh Manor) in 1662. Margaret was active in the family business as a seventeenth century travelogue shows [DAN]. One source, "Tales of the Old Dutch Graveyard" [COLL], appears to confuse Margaret with Philipse's second wife, Catherine.

De Vries Field is accessed via Devries Avenue in Philipse Manor. Both De Vries Field and the neighboring land of the General Motors plant were submerged areas of the ancient harbor once known as *Slapershaven*.

The field includes two ballfields and some newly constructed features: horse shoe pits, picnic shelter, bocce court, and playground. The lower reaches of the Pocantico River border the picnic area. The river's lower course was changed during the twentieth century.

See The Marsh and Donohue Field.

VAR: *Devries Ave Park, DeVries Field Park, Devries Park.*

Sergeant John Dean
Single-handedly fighting the Cowboys. Detail from *Hinton's Tales of the Neutral Ground*.

REF: CECGE:48; COLL:4; DAN:5,12,14,22,27,30,36,37,39,42,53,62,63, 65,77,85,103,104,105,106,116,154,279,35,362-365; HIS:8; NO:np; NOR:np; SM; SH:158; ST; TN [Aug. 2 1996].

Dean Park

This was the name of the Tarrytown park which occupied the southwest corner of Broadway and Main Street for ten years (1914-1923). It was located on the site of the old Dean house and store. The land was loaned to the Village of Tarrytown by Edward W. Harden, a newspaperman who worked for the *New York Times*. Harden had purchased the property from members of the Dean family. The Women's Civic League formed a committee, headed by Mrs. Fred J. Hall, to collect contributions for construction of the park. Between 1900 and 1912, a Mrs. Lowe operated the Far and Near Tea Room in the Dean house.

The heroic exploits of Sergeant John Dean are recorded in the *Souvenir of the Revolutionary Soldiers' Monument Dedication* [RA]. Dean was one of the first postmasters of the area. His son, Thomas, operated a general store at this location which became something of a local institution. Washington Irving, writing from Spain to his young niece, joked that the Queen of Spain might want to trade places with her if the queen had ever experienced the simple pleasures of Tarrytown life, or "...shopped at Tommy Dean's...." According to a column by Wally Buxton in the *Tarrytown Daily News* [DA], President Martin Van Buren stopped at the Dean store on January 22, 1839.

The Dean house on Main Street was not actually built by John Dean; it was purchased by Dean from George Combs.

VAR: Harden's Park.
REF: CA:291; DA [June 10 1975], [Apr. 23 1914], [Nov. 6 1994[pic]]; HIS:14-15; M22; RA:60-78; SC:205,239; TA:16,37; TARR:np[& pic]; TN [Dec. 20 1996], [Oct. 31. 1996]

Dearman*

This nineteenth century hamlet south of the Tarrytown area was later incorporated into the Village of Irvington. Justus Dearman, who bought the land from William Dutcher in 1812, sold it to a developer in 1850. Dearman died in 1855 at the age of ninety-one; he was buried in the Old Dutch Burying Ground of Sleepy Hollow.

The name of the hamlet was changed to Irvington in the mid-

1850s in honor of Washington Irving. Irvington was officially incorporated as a village in 1872.
VAR: Dearman's.
REF: CON:34; HIS:26; IN:50;Wes [FAL 1991,p.78]; WO:np.

Depot Plaza

The area surrounding Tarrytown's railroad station is known as Depot Plaza. This piece of real estate was actually created by nineteenth century landfill operations. Previously most of the area was submerged, a part of Tarrytown Bay. Further landfilling in the twentieth century created the parking area and recreational fields west of the tracks. The place name came into use sometime after the advent of the Hudson River railroad line about 1848.

See Losee Field.
VAR: Depot Square.
REF: CA:13; COR:2,21; DA [Dec.7 1994]; DA2 [Mar. 12 1937 pic]; NORT:4; RA:11; TA:65; TARR:np.

Detmer Estate

This property previously known as the Sigafus Estate, is now the site of the Edgemont Condominiums. Julian Francis Detmer (1865-1958) accumulated a portion of his wealth in the wool trade as a merchant and importer. In later years, he was a director of the County Trust Company, president of Detmer Securities Corporation, and proprietor of Detmer Nurseries. His interest in horticulture led him to win many prizes in that field. But some of the fine specimens which adorned his estate could have been planted in the days of a previous owner, Colonel James M. Sigafus.

In the years immediately after Detmer's death, the estate was a favorite spot for Sunday strolls. In winter, children would visit the place with their sleds.

The writer recalls that during the late 1960s "Detmer's Castle" was used briefly as a rectory during the construction of the new Church of the Transfiguration. In the early 1970s, the old but unique residence was torn down to make way for the Edgemont Condominium development. In 1997, Detmer's name still appeared on one of the pillars at the gate at the corner of Prospect and Benedict.

See Edgemont, the Pine Tree Lot, Wolf Hill, Sigafus Estate.
VAR: Detmer Castle, Detmer's.

REF: CA:237; DA2 [Mar. 13 1943]; GE:30; NE [Nov. 27 1958   29:2]; ST; TA:map; TAR:6; WES:Vol.34:16; WWW Vol 3.

Donohue Field

Father William J. Donohue was pastor of Saint Teresa's Church in the 1930s. About 1951, an athletic field was constructed and dedicated to Father Donohue at the "Marsh." This lay just down the hillside from Howard Street and stretched south from the west end of Continental Street. The North Tarrytown High School teams used this field for their home games. It included a baseball field, track, softball fields, tennis courts, a football and soccer field, girl's hockey field and basketball court. In the early 1960s General Motors purchased the land in order to extend its parking lot.

On a recent visit to Peabody Field, the writer noticed a small monument erected to the memory of Father Donohue. It is located between the parking area and Route 9 near the entrance to the park. The plaque reads, "This playground is dedicated to the memory of Rev. William Donohue, S. T. D., Pastor of St. Teresa's Church, 1925-1941, Donohue Field. In tribute to the man whose consecrated devotion to youth led to its inception and inspired its completion." It seems that this marker was relocated to Peabody Field sometime after Donohue Field ("the Marsh Field") was sold to General Motors. An uninformed observer could easily assume that Peabody Field was Donohue Field.

See Marsh Field.
REF: CA:253; CR; DA2 [Sept. 28 1932]; GA; SM; TAR:44.

Douglas Estate, the

Local maps of the 1870s show the Douglas estate located immediately north of the Thayer residence (Edgewood) and east of Gorey Brook Road.

See Prospect Hill, Douglas Park, Long View.
REF: CA:234; HU:176,178[pics]; M37; M40; M41.

Douglas Park

This Village of Sleepy Hollow park was named for stockbroker John Douglas (d. 1883). John Douglas was the brother of Henry L. Douglas, who owned the adjoining land in the 1880s.

The Douglas mansion stood on the hill above the park.

According to Hutchinson, Henry L. Douglas occupied the mansion from the 1880s until about 1900. The Douglas estate was inherited by William Harris Douglas, who owned it until the 1940s.

William Harris Douglas, a former congressman, acquired land from the John Webber estate. He gave the parcel to the Village of North Tarrytown on June 16, 1939. It was dedicated as Douglas Park on June 6, 1942. Douglas was quoted as saying, "I just thought it would come in nice for the people of North Tarrytown...."

The old Croton Aqueduct and the Pocantico River border the seventeen-acre park, east and west. The park features a small playground, picnic sites overlooking the Pocantico River, and dramatic, steep terrain descending to the river. The main access is from New Broadway.

See Prospect Hill, Long View, Webber Park.

REF: *A Plaque at Douglas Park; AR 1883 CA:234; DA2 [June 13 1942]; HU:176; M20:26; M21; M41; M47; M45; M58; MO:28; NO:np; SE 29; SL:map; TAR:44.*

Earlston

In 1890, this was the nineteen-acre estate of Mrs. A. M. Patterson. It stood on Woodland Avenue, off Cobb Lane. The estate extended beyond the top of the hillside, to where the Upper Lake now lies. The mansion stood east of the intersection of Wilson Park Drive and Beech Lane, just north of Pleasance, the W. S. Wilson residence. [See the map of 1891, M40.]

In the first half of the nineteenth century the land had been part of the Caleb (possibly Caleb, Jr.) Wildey holdings.

REF: *M34; M35; M40.*

East Tarrytown*

East Tarrytown was an alternate name for East View. Maps of 1881 in Hutchinson's *Storm's Bridge* [HUT] and Bolton's history of Westchester County [BOL] identify East Tarrytown as a hamlet lying just west of the Saw Mill River on the County House Road (Lower Cross Road). The tracks of the New York City and Northern Railroad are also shown as passing through East Tarrytown. The name does not appear in the first edition of Bolton (1848), but it can be found in the second (1881).

According to Scharf [SC], the place was formerly called

Knapp's Corners.
   See East View, Knapp's Corners.
REF: AB:88,[map];   BOL:vol.I,549;   LE:45;   M39;   M63;   SC:312;
   TWO:160; YE:np.

East View*

East View, apparently named for its impressive view of the Saw Mill River Valley, is not strictly in the Tarrytowns, but the hamlet which once stood there was closely associated with this community from Revolutionary days.

The farms and stores of East View are now gone, but the land is still nestled in the valley of the Saw Mill River east of the Tarrytown Lakes. Formerly known as East Tarrytown and Knapp's Corners, East View appears as a station stop on a New York and Northern Railway schedule of May 27, 1893. The county almshouse stood near this location from 1828 until the early 1900s. Canning and Buxton [CA] write that the settlement was once a "thriving agricultural and dairy center." They add that by 1920 John D. Rockefeller, Sr., had purchased most of East View and had the buildings removed. In 1930, John D. Rockefeller, Jr., donated land at East View for parkway construction. Today, there is an East View exit from the Saw Mill River Parkway in this area.

   See East Tarrytown, Knapp's Corners.
VAR: Eastview.
REF: CA:68,193,316 ; DA2 [May 24 1937], [Sept. 21 1942]; DE:4; HIS:38; HU:216; M40; M41; OW:23; WES:Vol.32, No. 4; YE:np.

Edgemont

Colonel James M. Sigafus purchased his estate (or a portion of it) from Alexander A. Meldrum on April 8, 1882. It appears that Sigafus named the place Edgemont. The estate was located on the south side of Prospect Avenue, west of Benedict Avenue in Tarrytown.

Scharf writes that Sigafus was a Civil War veteran who developed extensive ranching and silver mining interests in Colorado. He built a large mansion at Edgemont, which offered beautiful views of the Hudson River; the residence was completed in March of 1884. Scharf [SC] adds, "In style the house is a French villa with piazzas twelve feet wide around the entire building. It is constructed of pressed brick made at Glenn's Fall [*sic.*], New York, with terra-cotta trimmings, of which it took sixteen car-loads to finish the edifice. There is said to be more terra-cotta in this house than in any other in the United States. The granite columns are from the granite quarry at Quincy, Massachusetts."

Julian Detmer subsequently purchased the estate. In recent years, condominiums have been built there. Today, the name Edgemont still appears on one of the pillars at Prospect and Benedict.

See Detmer Estate, Wolf Hill, the Pine Tree Lot, Sigafus Estate.

REF: *CA:237; CAL1; SC:245; AR [May 5 1883], [Apr. 7 1887]; WES:Vol.34:16.*

Edgewood

The late nineteenth century estate of businessman-poet Stephen Henry Thayer lay northeast of where Gorey Brook Road intersects the Croton Aqueduct. The place was south of the Douglas Estate on Prospect Hill and north of Ridge Street. Thayer's collected poems are titled, *Songs of Sleepy Hollow*.

REF: *CA:234; HU:178; MO:27; M40; M41; WA:4, 17.*

Elmbrook

This estate had previously been part of Timothy C. Eastman's estate, Millbrook. It lay north of Lyndhurst and south of Paulding Avenue. It was owned (c.1917) by Allan S. Lehman, who had a new Tudor mansion designed and constructed. This mansion was demolished in 1978.

See Millbrook.

REF: *TA: map; ZU:88.*

Ericstan

This was an estate established by John Herrick. The mansion, alternately called "The Castle" or "Herrick's Folly," overlooked Rose Hill.

See Castle Ridge.

REF: *ZU:97.*

Farcus Hott*

This was a secret place used by patriots during the American Revolution. Also known as Kay's Cave, Farcus Hott served as a place of safety from the depredations of the "Neutral Ground." It is located on Beaver Hill, south of Route 119 and west of the Saw Mill River.

See picture in Hutchinson [HU]. See Beaver Hill.

REF: HUT:33,34[pic],35; M66; RA:112.

Forty Acre Lot, the

This forty-acre lot was located in today's Philipse Manor. The giant Indian Chestnut Tree, Hokohongus, once stood here.

See Hokohongus and Philipse Manor.

REF: BA:30; CA:18.

Four Corners, The*

The Four Corners is a name popularized by James Fenimore Cooper in *The Spy*. This was the location of the tavern operated by his character, Betsy Flanagan, who is said to have invented the "cocktail" during the Revolution. Betsy Flanagan's tavern may be styled after the historic tavern which once stood at Youngs' Corners.

See Youngs' Corners, The Burnt House.

VAR: *Upper Corners, The Corners.*

REF: HIN:274,275; HUF:255,256,324; MI:17; SC:312; WE:205,206; SH:461; YE:np.

Fountain Square

A square formerly located at the intersection of Wildey Street, Central Avenue, and Valley Street was known by this name. The fountain was dedicated in 1891 to the memory of Frederick G. LeRoy, a local doctor. Information here is sketchy, but it appears that Mrs. William H. Gihon and/or her daughter Mrs. LeRoy (Caroline R. Gihon) donated a fountain at this place, dedicated to Mrs. LeRoy's husband. Dr. Frederick G. LeRoy was killed in a riding accident in front of the old Florence Inn about 1889. In 1933 Fountain Square was renamed Columbus Square.

After her husband's death, Mrs. LeRoy, bought a home on North Broadway, which was to become the headquarters for the Woman's Civic League of the Tarrytowns from 1920 to 1937. Today Dywer Funeral Home is located in the building.

REF: CA:136,237; DA2 [Mar. 12 1937], [June 13 1942]; TA:65; TARR:np[& pic].

Francis Core's Homestead Lot

This was a name for the Upper Mills in the early 1850s. The writer has no information on Francis Core. Lossing [LO] relates that, in the spring of 1860, Philipse Castle passed into the hands of a "Mr. Storm." He adds that prior to Storm's ownership "the Castle" had remained in the hands of the Beekman family for about seventy-five years. This seems to imply that, if Core did own the place during the 1850s, he was a member of the Beekman family.
REF: *HU:94; LO:327; M44.*

Fremont Fountain

This fountain is located on the east side of Route 9, opposite Peabody Field. It was created in the early twentieth century by James Ceconi, a local craftsman. The fountain was commissioned by William Rockefeller and dedicated to his former neighbor, John C. Frémont. It is the last of the many public fountains which were formerly located in the two villages to refresh horses and travelers.

See Cold Spring Fountain, Fremont Pond.
VAR: *Fremont Bowl and Fountain, Fremont Bowl*
REF: *AL:154; HU:86,87[pic],88[pic]; ST.*

Fremont Pond

This pond is named for John C. "The Pathfinder" Frémont (1813-1890), former owner of Pokahoe. Frémont's estate was a ninety-five-acre parcel covering today's Sleepy Hollow Manor. Frémont distinguished himself early in his military career during expeditions into the West. In 1843, accompanied by the famous scout Kit Carson, he completed the mapping of the Oregon Trail. Frémont was instrumental in securing California for the United States and served briefly as one of that state's first two United States senators. He was the first Republican candidate for president (1856) and a high-ranking Union general during the Civil War. From 1878 to 1883 he was governor of the territory of Arizona. His wife, Jessie Hart Benton, was the daughter of Senator Thomas Hart Benton. Motivated by Frémont's financial reverses, she became a popular writer late in life to help support her family.

See Pokahoe.
VAR: *Freemont Pond, Lake Fremont, Fremont's Pond.*
REF: *CA:171; GE:4; GR:52; HU:86; LE:53 ; M19; MI:21; TN [Dec. 13 1996].*

Fremont Spring

This spring, also known as Cold Spring, is the source of Fremont Fountain and Fremont Pond. Today it passes down the hill from Sleepy Hollow Cemetery, crosses beneath Route 9, and continues along the south edge of Peabody Field and on down to Fremont Pond. The water empties from the pond into the *Hafentje*, a small bay which looks more like a swamp today. From the *Hafentje*, the water moves into the Hudson River.

See Fremont Pond, Fremont Fountain, Cold Spring.

REF: CH:No. 4 Sept 1959 [page 5].

Gebney Brook

A tributary of the Pocantico, this seems to be identical with the Rockefeller Brook, intersecting Sleepy Hollow Road approximately a quarter of a mile south of the Carl Brook. Bacon [BA] reports that this was a good stream for fishing in the mid-nineteenth century. [See map of Tarrytown Heights Co. 1871, M36].

Gebney may be an early variation of the name Gibney. That family had holdings in the Pocantico Hills area during the nineteenth century. John Gibney owned a large farm there in 1871. [See M36.]

The name may also be a corruption of the name Gedney. According to the *Tarrytown Daily News* [DA] of September 30, 1992, Warren F. Gedney of Port Chester, who died the age of 79, was the last of a long line of Westchester County residents of that name. All were said to be descended from John and Mary Gedney, who landed in Salem, Massachusetts, in 1637. Absalom Gedney was a tenant of Philipsburgh at the time of the Revolution.

See Rockefeller Brook.

REF: BA:60; DA [Sept 1992]; EA:107; M36; ST.

General Motors Site, the

This is the land on which the General Motors factory stands in the Village of Sleepy Hollow. Part of the Kingsland Point portion of this site was used for automobile manufacturing as early as 1900. The original plant was designed by Stanford White. The first gas powered cars made here were manufactured by Maxwell-Briscoe from 1904-1913. This firm then merged with United States Motor Company, but that company soon went out of business due to financial trouble.

In June 1914, a rising new car company named Chevrolet

purchased the Maxwell-Briscoe plant for $267,000. Chevrolet then gained control of the General Motors Company. In 1918, General Motors and Chevrolet merged under the name of General Motors Corporation. The plant permanently ceased to do machine work at the site after a serious fire in 1919. In the 1920s, GM claimed and filled in 7.97 acres of land from the ancient harbor once known as *Slapershaven*. Barges were sunk in the bay at the Pocantico River mouth, and sediment was pumped in behind them. A new administration building and assembly plant were completed in 1930, replacing the original Stanford White and Maxwell-Briscoe structures. Over the decades expansion of the plant and site continued.

Late in the 1950s GM purchased 29.5 acres of marshland which had been used as a recreational field by the Village of North Tarrytown (Sleepy Hollow). In 1960, after receiving a New York State land grant of Hudson River bottom, the company filled in an additional 15.7 acre stretch along its western shoreline, bringing the mainland even closer to the Tarrytown Lighthouse.

In 1992, GM announced that the North Tarrytown (Sleepy Hollow) plant would close three years later. On June 28, 1996, the plant at North Tarrytown (Sleepy Hollow) was finally shut down. The demolition of the plant was scheduled to begin in early 1997. See TN, May 31, 1996, for an extensive article on GM and its closing.

See Kingsland Point.

VAR: *the GM Site; the GM site.*
REF: *CRA:[pic]; DA2 [Apr. 16 1942]; GM:3,8-14,19,22,23,26-34,44- 45,50,55, 56,69,97,99,100,113-115 pics; ST; TARR:[pic]; TN [Nov. 22 1996 & pic], [Aug. 16 1996], [July 26 1996 pic], [June 7 1996 & pic], [May 31 1996 & pics.], [Apri.12 1996 & pic],[Nov. 16 1995 & pic].*

Glenmary

George Lewis, Jr., owned this estate which occupied the area known today as Tappan Landing. The twenty-three-acre estate was south of Church Street and west of Broadway. As a civic gesture in 1891, Lewis and his family donated a large "Medallion vase" as a decoration for Depot Plaza. The Lewis estate was later purchased by Robert Clowery, an early president of Western Union.

See Tappan Landing.
REF: *CA:235; M40; SC:pic. opp. 232.*

Glenloch

The former estate of J. T. Law was more than fifty acres in extent. It now constitutes part of the Rockefeller holdings. The place was situated west of the junction of Sleepy Hollow Road and Webber Avenue and north of Bedford Road. According to Scharf [SC], the estate stretched 1,100 feet along Bedford Road and 1,700 feet along the "old Sleepy Hollow Road." A successful New York lawyer, Law purchased his estate in 1869 from John W. Patterson.

See the estate of D. S. Law in M37.

VAR: *Glen Loch.*
REF: *CA:296; M37; M40; SC:305.*

Glenville*

Glenville is an unincorporated Greenburgh hamlet lying along Benedict Avenue, near its intersection with Tarrytown Road. Canning writes that, commercially, this settlement grew up around quarrying activities, and the name is derived from the glen which stretches from Hackley hill to Elmsford. S. J. Sackett maintained a granite quarry there in the late nineteenth century. The growth of the settlement seems to have been stimulated by the construction of Benedict Avenue in the middle of the nineteenth century.

The name Glenville appears on maps as early as 1868, but it may have been in use earlier. See TN for Paul Feiner's letter concerning woodland space in Glenville.

REF: *CA:99,314; DA2 [Dec. 7 1929]; HU:162; HUT:76[map]; M39; TN [Aug. 23 1996], [June 7 1996 & pic].*

Glenwode Park

Glenwode Park is a twentieth century residential development. It is located south of Sheldon Avenue, close to where that street meets Broadway. Today, a sign on Walter Street marks the district. Just south of this, a sign on Broadway indicates an estate called Glenwode. Both of these places were formerly parts of Graystone.

See Graystone.

VAR: *Glenwode.*
REF: *CA:238; TAR:40.*

Goat Hill

Hudson Street passes along the top of Goat Hill. This low rise

overlooking the Hudson River, near the bottom of Beekman Avenue, was named for the goats which once grazed there.
REF: CA:91.

Gorey Brook
This tributary of the Pocantico River is said to have been the site of a bloody Revolutionary War engagement. Gorey Brook rises in Briarcliff Manor and connects with the Pocantico River and the valley of Sleepy Hollow just within the northern border of the Village of Sleepy Hollow The name can be found on a map of 1891 (M40).
VAR: Gory Brook, Gorey Creek.
REF: HU:9,47; LE:57; M40; M19; M29; M45; M65; WES:Vol.32, No. 4.

Gracemere
Gracemere is a Pennybridge estate which once belonged to Charles Graef about 1891. It is located at the south end of Browning Lane. The writer, who often visited Gracemere during the 1950s, can recall that the mansion was divided into two or three apartment units. The pond below the main building was used for wading and rowboating.
REF: M35; M40.

Graystone
This was the summer residence of millionaire Walter S. Gurnee, who died in 1905, leaving an estate of $8,986,654. His house had been built about 1850 by David M. Steubins. The property subsequently belonged to Mrs. Josiah Macy (Caroline Everit Macy, 1839-1899). Her husband Josiah Macy (1838-1876) was the son of William H. Macy and the grandson of sea captain Josiah Macy (1785-1872), both of whom established the successful shipping and commission house of Josiah Macy & Son. The younger Josiah was an early stockholder and an official of the Standard Oil Company. Mrs. Macy's one hundred-acre estate lay along the east side of Broadway, between land belonging to Jay Gould on the south and Sheldon Road on the north; on the east lay Gracemere.

Mrs. Macy's son, Valentine Everit Macy (1871-1931), resided in Ossining (Scarborough) and was elected superintendent of the county poor in 1914. He used some of his private fortune to spearhead innovative programs in public welfare, playing an important role in establishing a separate county hospital and almshouse and a penitentiary for first offenders. Later, Macy served as president of the county parks commission.

His son was Josiah Noel Macy (1900-1977), whose family sold its interests in several Westchester newspapers to the Gannett Company in 1964. The Macy family also owned radio station WFAS.

VAR: Greystone.
REF: CA:105,212,214; DA2 [Aug. 8 1930]; DI:Vol.4,178-179; M35; M40; NE [Dec. 29 1871 2:2],[May 22 1948 23:2],[Sept. 26 1905 9:6]; SC:245; WWW (Historical Vol.).

Greenburgh, The Town of

The name Greenburgh is said to derive from the Dutch word, *grein*, for grain. Greenburgh was one of twenty-one Westchester towns (townships) created by New York State in 1788. Mount Pleasant was also created at this time. The act creating New York's townships had long term implications for this community. It meant that a place which had historically viewed itself as a single community would be split by a seemingly arbitrary border. What we know today as the Village of Sleepy Hollow became part of the Town of Mount Pleasant, while lands which, eighty-two years later, would constitute the Village of Tarrytown were incorporated into the Township of Greenburgh.

The new township border at André Brook probably had little immediate influence on the daily life of the community. However, it was to have more concrete implications as time went by, particularly in the late nineteenth century when the two villages elected to incorporate. Prior to the Revolutionary War, the areas north and south of André Brook had been parts of a larger political subdivision of Westchester County known as Philipsburgh Manor; this unit had encompassed modern day Mount Pleasant, Greenburgh, and Yonkers.

At this date it is difficult to determine what interests influenced the drawing of the Greenburgh/Mount Pleasant boundary. It may have been governed by a wish to keep the large Beekman holdings intact. The lower portion of André Brook constituted the southern border of the Gerard Beekman holdings, and it is along this line that the township border was drawn. At that time, title to all of this land had just been sold by the auction of Philipsburgh Manor. The lands had been seized from Frederick Philipse III by the newly created State of

New York. Those governing the division may have wished to follow certain natural features on which the division of tenant farms had historically been based.

In addition to Tarrytown, Greenburgh includes the villages of Hastings-on-Hudson, Elmsford, Dobbs Ferry, Irvington, Ardsley, Hartsdale, and certain unincorporated areas of the township.

REF: BOL:Map.[equated with Elmsford]; HI:19; HIST:179; M21; M49; MI:19; SH:531,611; TA:15; TAR:7; YE:np.

Greensburgh

This was an early nineteenth century name for the hamlet of Tarrytown. In "The Legend of Sleepy Hollow" the narrator states "...there lies a small market-town or rural port, which by some is called Greensburgh, but which is more generally and popularly known as Tarry Town." Maps of 1835 and 1846 refer to the hamlet of Tarrytown as "Greensburgh or Tarry Town." See M59 and M60.

In the early nineteenth century some may have considered the incorporation of the Town of Greenburgh in 1788 to supersede the local names of certain places like Tarrytown. Today, only unincorporated areas of a township are commonly referred to by the township's name. It should be noted that the Village of Dobbs Ferry was originally incorporated under the name of Greenburgh, but then changed back to Dobbs Ferry.

REF: IR:21; M32; M59; M60.

Hackley Hill

Hackley Hill is a high rise of ground previously known as Waldheim. The hill is named for Hackley School, which in turn was named for Mrs. Caleb Brewster Hackley (d. 1913). Mrs. Hackley opened a boys' school on Castle Ridge in 1899. The school subsequently acquired Waldheim where the school is located today.

It should be noted that Lederer [LE] assumes the present school was built on the estate of Mrs. Hackley; this is not the case. Mrs. Hackley lived near Marymount Avenue.

VAR: Hackley hill.
REF: CA:314; LE:61.

Hafentje, the

This is as cove or small harbor on the Hudson River. It lies immediately to the west of Fremont Pond and north of the Yellow Rocks. The *Hafentje* is today more like a marsh, and it is enclosed by the railroad line on its west side. The name is said to derive from Dutch times, meaning literally "the small harbor, or cove." This differentiates the *Hafentje* from the Pocantico River mouth, *Slapershaven* (literally, sleepers harbor). Bacon suggests that the American "Water Guard" of the Revolutionary War made forays from the *Hafentje* and *Slapershaven*. He also alludes to the legend of a ghost ship or Flying Dutchman which was supposed to skirt the *Hafentje* and *Slapershaven*.

Revolutionary War soldier Stephen Van Tassel (b. 1758) settled on lands bordering the Hafentje. He saw action at the Battle of White Plains and Youngs' House, among other engagements. In 1780 he was captured and imprisoned in one of New York's notorious Sugar House prisons for nearly a year.

Like *Slapershaven*, the *Hafentje*'s connection to the Hudson has been largely obstructed by the railroad since about 1848. [See M34.]

See Slaeperingh Haven.
VAR: Hafenje, Hovelchie [M65], Havenje; Haventje, Hobbinger.
REF: BA:76; BAC:216,241; BO:348; BOL:vol.I,547; CAS; M34; M65; RA:121,122; SC:310.

Halleston

Halleston was the Tappan Hill estate of Wall Street businessman Jacques S. Halle and his wife, Clara. The mansion, later to became the home of Tappan Hill Restaurant, was built by the Halles in 1915.

Halleston's lands were bordered by Rose Hill Avenue, Highland Avenue, Benedict Avenue, and Union Avenue. The driveway entrance was from the corner of Rosehill Avenue and Benedict Avenue; the old pillars can still be found at this location. All of Altamont Avenue was formerly part of Halleston. After Mrs. Clara Halle's death in 1941, the estate was purchased by the company of developer David Swope, and the mansion became a restaurant. Today the mansion is occupied by a catering business.

Prior to the Halles' acquisition of the estate, it belonged to Charles Gardiner, an attorney, who occupied it from 1904-1915. Gardiner bought the property from the famous American author, Mark Twain (Samuel Clemens, 1835-1910), who owned the estate from 1902-1904. Earlier, the southern twenty-acre parcel of the estate was owned by Captain W. Casey, and the northern twenty-acre parcel was owned by a Captain Edward Cobb [See more about Cobb under Cobb's Lot].

See Hillcrest and Tappan Hill.

REF: CA:233; CON:36; DA[Apr. 4 1942,p.1]; GET:14; M35; TA:map; TARR:np.

Hart's Mills

Hart's Mills was located on the Pocantico River, just above the Carl Brook tributary. The place was called by this name in 1867 or earlier. George Hart was designated as a landowner here in 1877 [M65]. The mill house was in ruins by the 1890s. Hutchinson suggests that it may have been the site of a Philipse mill in the colonial period.

This mill has at times been confused with Carl's Mill.

REF: HU:22,105,165,166[pics],M35; M65.

Hart's Pond

This was the mill pond at Hart's Mills. In 1874 it appeared on the incorporation map for the Village of North Tarrytown (Sleepy Hollow). The mill was located just west of the intersection of Sleepy Hollow Road and the northern village line. Only the southern tip of the pond was within the village limits. This lower end of the pond appears to have moved further north in a map of 1893 [M41]. A North Tarrytown village map of 1877 [M65] outlines the borders of both "Hart's Old Pond" and the "New Pond." The pond no longer exists.

See Hart's Mills.

REF: HU:100; M28; M41; M65.

Hawksrest

See Malkasten.

REF: AND:34.

Headless Horseman Bridge, the

This is another name for the Sleepy Hollow Bridge. See Sleepy Hollow Bridge, Washington Irving Memorial Bridge.

REF: CA:47;   CAL1;   CON:20;   CRA:81;   HA:65,102;   HIS:10; HU:112[cap],252;   JE:381;   MO:27;   OW:12;   PE1:   vol.24/3

Hokohongus
Probably after the turn of the twentieth century when it was killed by the chestnut blight. Courtesy Westchester County Historical Society.

326,333,334; PH:np; PHI:np; RO:np,22; ST; TARR:np [& pic]; TN [Oct. 31 1996 & pic], [July 12 1996 & pic].

Highland Turnpike, the
See Albany Post Road.
VAR: Highland Turnpike Road, the.

Hillcrest
This was the twenty-acre estate of Captain W. C. Casey on Tappan Hill. It later constituted the southern half of Halleston. A map of 1891 in HUT shows the property to be north of Benedict Avenue, east of Rosehill Avenue, and west of Highland Avenue. The land extended roughly from where Tappan Hill Restaurant stands today, to Benedict Avenue.
See Halleston, Tappan Hill.
REF: CA:232-233; CON:36; M35; M40.

Hillside
The estate of Sanford Cobb stood on the south side of Cobb Lane, east of the aqueduct. By 1881 [M18] the land belonged to "Mrs. A. A. Cobbs [sic]."
REF: M18; M38; M56.

Hokohongas
This is a celebrated chestnut tree which stood in what is now Philipse Manor. Local historian Edgar Mayhew Bacon wrote, "the great tree with its twenty feet girth lifts a coronal of plumes in the center of the forty acre lot." The tree died of the chestnut blight early in this century.

Hokohongus is reputed to have had a special significance for the Indians of the area. Some suggest that it marked a burying ground; others that it was a meeting place for councils and treaties. Still others suggest that it served as an focus for the celebration of the harvest.

According to Leslie Verne Case, "Ho Kohongus" was not only the name of the notable tree, but also the name of an Indian village which was located in today's Philipse Manor. Case was a leading member of the Historical Society of the Tarrytowns and the Westchester Historical Society's chairman on Indian remains in the 1930s. He wrote that there were three local Indian villages along the banks of the Hudson: AlisKong, Ho Kohongus, and Pokerhoe. The lands of the first were south of the Pocantico; to the north was the village called Ho Kohongus where Philipse Manor lies, and then there was Pokerhoe in the area of today's Sleepy Hollow Manor. Unfortunately, Mr. Case does not offer his sources.

Case classifies Hokohongas as an American Chestnut tree (*Castanea dentata*) with a height of one hundred feet and a circumference of thirty feet. He reports it was the largest tree in Westchester County, perhaps even New York State.

The dead tree was still standing as late as 1913, but during the course of this century its precise location was forgotten. Joseph Lillis, a Philipse Manor resident, has retreived this information for us. By cross-referencing maps, deeds, and photographs of Philipse Manor, Lillis has located the site of the ancient tree about 150-200 feet west of Bellwood Avenue, roughly midway between Millard and Highland Avenues.

VAR: *Hokohongus*, also known as the Indian Chestnut Tree, *Ho Kohongus*, *Hokohongas*.
REF: BA:30; CA:8; CON:7,24,27,np.; HU:7,9; MO:1; TN [Aug. 23 1996 & pic], [Aug. 30 1996]; WES:6:42-44.

Hollow, the

An early published source for this name is found in Irving's essay, "Sleepy Hollow." (See IRVING. This essay is not to be confused with Irving's famous story, "The Legend of Sleepy Hollow.") In Irving's essay, "the Hollow" is used as a synonym for all of Sleepy Hollow.

The name also applies specifically to that low portion of Broadway near the Old Dutch Church and the Sleepy Hollow Bridge. Bolton referred to the area by this name as early as 1848, and it is still called "the Hollow" today by some long-time residents.

In Irving's "Wolfert's Roost," this place name is frequently used as a nickname for the place name "Sleepy Hollow." Note that the narrator of "The Legend of Sleepy Hollow" describes Ichabod's flight from the Headless Horseman as leading along the lower route through a "sandy hollow."

See Sleepy Hollow.
REF: BOL:vol.1,526,532,546; CON:29; HIS:10; HU:64; IR:311,46; IRVING:8; ST; TWO:62.

Holmes Brook

This brook marked the southern boundary of the 280-acre farm purchased by George Comb and James Hammond. They bought the land from the New York State Commissioners of Forfeiture about 1785. The brook is unnamed on the map of land sales. [M1, M6]. It is also unnamed in a later map of 1867 [M35], where it is shown running to the Hudson just south of Church Street.

The brook rises near the intersection of Highland and Benedict Avenues. Crossing to the west side of Benedict Avenue, it forms a pond in front of the Christian Science Church. Ice was harvested from the pond in the mid-nineteenth century.

Holmes Brook is named for Nathaniel B. Holmes, a book merchant who founded Christ Episcopal Church in 1836. According to Bolton [BOL], Holmes came to Tarrytown in 1833. Finding no Episcopal Church, he applied to his bishop for permission to "lay-read" and to engage a place in which to do so. He received permission to use the Asbury Methodist Episcopal Church on Sunday afternoons from the trustees of that congregation. According to Canning [CA], Reverend John Barnet Matthias founded the Asbury M. E. Church after coming to the Tarrytown area in 1796. It later became the United Methodist Church of the Tarrytowns on South Washington Street.

Holmes was also a founder of the Westchester County Savings Bank in 1853, and he served as its president and treasurer. Washington Irving served on the board of this institution.

See Alipconck Brook. See Holmes Point.

REF: AR [Apri. 22 1882]; BOL:vol.I,298; CA:246; LE:69; M1; M6; SC:232; TA:41; TN [Oct. 31 1996].

Holmes Point

" The Point, into the Hudson River just north of the Tappan Zee Bridge, is named for Nathaniel B. Holmes, who in 1835 retired from the book business in New York City, and the next year founded Christ Episcopal Church in Tarrytown." [Lederer in LE.]

The 1891 map in Canning [CA] shows the point to be on the south side of the mouth of Holmes Brook. The point was part of Glenmary, the estate of George Lewis, Jr.

See Holmes Brook.

REF: CA:146; LE:69; M40.

Homestead, the

According to Scharf (1886), the Homestead lay between Broadway and the Old Croton Aqueduct, just north of the Grinnell estate. It was formerly the estate of Benson Ferris, who built a house there in 1835 after having sold his home called Wolfert's Roost to Washington Irving. His son, also named Benson, became the president of the National Bank of Tarrytown in the late nineteenth century.

The estate was subsequently owned by H. R. Worthington (1817-1880). Henry Rossiter Worthington was a hydraulic engineer and the inventor of steam pumps. He was president of Nason Manufacturing Company in New York and founder of the American Society of Mechanical Engineers.

See Northcote.

REF: *DI:Vol.X,p539; SC:242; TARR:np.*

Horseman's Trail, the

This is a portion of the Hudson River Greenway Trail running through the Village of Sleepy Hollow. Plans for the trail were put into motion by the summer of 1994, and it was opened in December 1995. Improvements were made by the Village of Sleepy Hollow recreation department throughout the following year.

The trail begins at De Vries Field and follows the Pocantico River upstream, along the vestiges of the ancient harbor known as *Slapershaven* in Dutch times. It then connects with Philipsburg Manor Restoration. Crossing Broadway at the Sleepy Hollow Bridge, it then proceeds into Sleepy Hollow Cemetery, traveling along the west side of the Pocantico River. The trail next crosses the river at the bridge leading to the new part of the cemetery and enters Douglas Park. From there hikers can connect with the Old Croton Aqueduct Trail which heads north into the Rockefeller Preserve, or south toward Sleepy Hollow High School. The Horseman's Trail is projected at some future time to link with Sleepy Hollow Landing, a one-acre village park at the Hudson River waterfront.

The name of the trail is a reference to the Headless Horseman of Sleepy Hollow, a well-known local ghost. This is not the traditional path of Ichabod Crane's flight from the Headless Horseman, but the ghost on horseback doubtlessly covered this ground as well during his midnight adventures.

VAR: *Horsemen's [sic] Trail; the Horseman's trail.*

REF: AT; DA [Nov. 1 1995]; NOR:np; PE2 [SUM,1994]; ST; TN [Nov. 30 1995], [July 19 1996 & pic], [July 12 1996 & pic], [June 7 1996], [Nov. 30 1995 & pic].

Hudson Pines

Hudson Pines is located to the west of Bedford Road where it swings past the mansion at Kykuit. This farm is owned by David Rockefeller (b. 1915), a son of John D. Rockefeller, Jr., and a brother of the late Vice President of the United States, Nelson Rockefeller. David served as chairman and chief executive officer of Chase Manhattan Corporation from 1969 to 1981.
REF: BI:np.

Hudson River, the

The Hudson River has been extremely important to the life and development of the Tarrytowns. The river is named for Henry Hudson, the English explorer who claimed the river valley for the Dutch in 1609. The Tarrytowns lie on a very wide section of the river known as the Tappan Zee.

The river does not seem to have been commonly known as the Hudson until the railroad made the name popular in the nineteenth century. However, there are occurrences of "Hudson's River" in records dating from the 1680s (see BOL).

See an article written by Susan Fenimore Cooper published in the Magazine of American History (quoted in IN).

VAR: Hudson's River, Hudson's river, North River, Mohicanittuk [Delaware], Mahikkannittuc, Shatamuc [Sint-Sinck], Cohohatatea [Iroquois], Mauritus [Dutch—for Prince Maurice of Orange]; Maurits Rivier, Manhattes, Manhattans Rivier, Noort Rivier, Norrdt Riviere, Groote Riviere, Groote Rivier, The Great River, Rio de Montagne, Montaigne Rivier, Rio de Gamas (Spanish).
REF: AC:11; BOL:vol.I,268; BOL:vol.II,592-593; DA2:np; DAI:31; LE:121; IN:18,19; IRVIN:106; M10; M16; OE:11-12; WO:8.

Irving

Prior to the incorporation of the Village of Tarrytown, the area around Van Wart and Paulding Avenues was known by this name. (Van Wart Avenue was then known as Franklin Avenue.) The name of this small hamlet was no doubt a homage to Washington Irving, a distinguished resident of the region. The place became more densely settled when Franklin and Paulding Avenues were constructed in 1836. This date is given by Lederer [LE] who writes that the poet, Minna Irving (no relation to Washington Irving), resided in this neighborhood.

Samuel Lyon of Yonkers refers to the place name Irving in an interview recorded by John M. MacDonald in 1845. A map of 1846 [M60] includes this place name.

REF: CA:64; LE:73; M38; M60; M62; MA:172.

Irving Memorial

This is a memorial by Daniel Chester French, dedicated in 1928 to Washington Irving. French is well known as the designer of the Lincoln statue in the Lincoln Memorial. The Irving Memorial stands at the corner of Sunnyside Lane and Broadway. It includes two bronze reliefs and a bust of Washington Irving. Mrs. Henry Black, an Irvington resident, donated the funds for the monument.

See Irving's Grave, Sleepy Hollow and Sunnyside, for more on Washington Irving.

VAR: *Washington Irving Memorial.*
REF: BU:80; CON:22,23.

Irving Park

A mid-nineteenth century etching shows Irving Park situated to the east of the Old Dutch Church and the Pocantico River. The park was to be a one hundred-acre residential development of "villas" or "cottages" designed by Charles H. Lyon, Esq. These residences were to be situated where Douglas Park, Webber Park and Cedar Hill are today. Lederer writes that three "kiosques" were the only structures ever completed. See Lossing [LOS] for more information and etchings.

REF: HU:89[pic]; LE:73; LO:327-330.

Irving's Grave

The grave of Washington Irving in Sleepy Hollow Cemetery is situated between the Old Dutch Church and the Battle Hill Monument. The site was declared a National Historic Monument in 1974.

Although best known for his light-hearted, masterfully crafted stories of the Hudson River Valley, "Rip Van Winkle" and "The Legend of Sleepy Hollow," Irving was a prolific writer of history, biography, and travelogue. He was America's first internationally acclaimed author. Irving spent a number of his adult years in England, where he wrote *The Sketch Book*. He also lived for many years in Spain as a writer and diplomat.

During his teenage years, Irving visited friends and relations in Tarrytown. Accompanied by his friend James K. Paulding he had opportunities to go on excursions through Sleepy Hollow in the valley of the Pocantico. Irving was trained as a lawyer, but never seriously practiced that profession. After a short and unsuccessful participation in the family export business, he took up the pen as his main calling. For many years he lived in Europe working in America's diplomatic corps, but when he returned to America, he was universally embraced for his literary achievements. In later years he purchased a home at Sunnyside, which became a favorite cultural destination for writers, artists, and dignitaries from around the world. Except for a short assignment as minister to Spain, Irving quietly lived out the final years of his life writing and entertaining at Sunnyside.

REF: COLL:29-30; HA:105; HARP:np[pic].

Jackson's Lot

This was a lot at the northwest corner of Beekman Avenue and Pocantico Street. The Van Tassel Apartment Building stands on this site today. The place was first known as Jackson's Lot sometime after 1869, when it became the playing field of Jackson Military Academy. The academy was founded in Danbury in 1854 by the Reverend Frederick J. Jackson, A. M. It was moved to the Beekman Avenue site in 1869.

Scharf [SC, 1886] records, "...Jackson's Military Institute, held in the large building on Beekman Avenue opposite the head of Cortlandt Street. It is the same building, enlarged and improved, that was occupied by the Irving Institute at the beginning of its career." Bolton's second edition [1881] reports, "The location is perhaps the most desirable that could be selected for the purposes of education in this vicinity." The Irving Institute, which preceded Jackson's Academy on the site, was established in 1838 by W. P. Lyon. For a time, David S. Rowe operated the Irving Institute from a new location on the corner of Pocantico and Howard Streets. See M56.

After the academy closed in 1880, the lot served as an unofficial public playground. Subsequently the site was purchased by the parish of St. Teresa in 1894, and the first St. Teresa's School stood there until 1927. According to a writer in TN, the lot was known for a time as St. Teresa lot. The Van Tassel Apartments, a residential project planned and funded by John D. Rockefeller, Jr., opened here in December of 1929. The complex is said to have been named after Katrina Van Tassel by Rockefeller's wife, Abby Aldrich Rockefeller.

VAR: *St. Teresa lot.*

REF: *BOL:vol.I,295; CA:89-90,149,154,164,253,273; DA [Dec. 7 1929]; DA2 [Dec. 7 1929]; HU:82,187[pic]; M18; M38; M56; SC:302; TN [July 26 1996], [Aug. 30 1996].*

Jacob Mott House, the

From the early eighteenth century until 1896 this house stood on the site of the old John Van Tassel farm. The parcel was purchased by Van Tassel after the Revolutionary War; he had been a tenant of Philipsburgh. The farm was 160 acres, extending from the Tarrytown Lots to Mekeel Avenue, then eastward to where the Tarrytown Lakes lie today.

Local tradition designates this place as the home of "Legend of Sleepy Hollow" character, Katrina Van Tassel. Irving's schoolmaster, Ichabod Crane, is said to have begun his fateful journey north along the Post Road from this spot. Bacon relates that Washington Irving's sister was a boarding guest at this place and that the author made frequent visits there. Bacon adds that Irving even interposed to prevent the owner from making alterations to the old house.

Somehow the house appeared a little too spare to serve as a model for the rustic affluence of Baltus Van Tassel's home. Some suggest that the Mott House may have served as only the location for Katrina's home, but that Irving's description was inspired by Philipse Castle. John Van Tassel did indeed have a daughter named Catherine who died in 1820 at the age of forty-eight. The *Tarrytown Centennial Album* [TARR] includes a photograph, taken at the time of the centennial, of a woman named Katrina Van Tassel. She is said to be a direct descendant of Katrina Van Tassel, the daughter of John Van Tassel.

The history of the house begins long before the Revolutionary period. It was built between 1712 and 1714 by Abraham Martling (1693-1761). Martling was a blacksmith who, for a time, served as justice of the peace and town clerk of Philipsburgh.

The structure was operated as a tavern during the Revolution under the proprietorship of Elizabeth Van Tassel; Elizabeth may have been a relation of John Van Tassel. It is said that an American force led by Major Hunt surprised a party of British soldiers at the Van Tassel Tavern. The British contingent were taking their refreshment and playing cards when a club-wielding Hunt fell upon them with his comrades. "Clubs are trumps!" cried Hunt. He offered the enemy soldiers good "quarter" and marched them off to captivity.

Later, after the farm was purchased by John Van Tassel (1737-1807), it was owned by Ralph Van Houter, Jr., then a Mr. Austin, then Jonathan Odell, then a Mr. Lamouroux. It then passed to the Mott family. Jacob L. Mott owned the southern portion of the farm; his son, Jacob Mott, own the northern portion which included the "Mott House."

In 1896, despite the objections of some local historians, the house was torn down, and the Washington Irving School was built on the site. Later the name was changed to Pierson School, and the name Washington Irving was given to a new high school at Broadway and Franklin Street. The latter Washington Irving School has since served as a junior high school and now a middle school. The Landmark Condominiums now occupy the old Pierson School building.

See Bacon [BA:88] for a drawing of the Jacob Mott House.

REF: *BA:131-135; HIS:39-40; SC:232; ST; WES:Vol.12,No.4,p.90-91,91[pic]*.

Jones Hill

This name appears in Bolton's 1848 edition [BO]. Bolton seems to imply that the name, Jones Hill, referred to the hill behind the Old Dutch Church [Battle Hill], whereas later writers understand Jones Hill to be the same as Cedar and Prospect Hills. Raymond also refers to the name in *Washington at Tarrytown* [1893].

The hill was named for Cornelius Jones who, according to Couzens' map, bought two hundred acres from the Commissioners of Forfeiture by the year 1785. According to this map, the Jones tract lay east of the Pocantico.

According to East [EA], before the Revolution, Cornelius Jones paid Frederick Philipse III 4 pounds, 4 shillings, 6 pence as a yearly rent for his tenant farm. The Jones farmhouse stood just north of the intersection of Sleepy Hollow Road and Webber Avenue [M6].

See Cedar Hill, Prospect Hill.
REF: BO:317; BOL:vol.I,506; EA:107; LE:74; M6; RAY:12.

Kaakoote
In the late nineteenth century this was the name of the W. B. Wadsworth estate. It lay where the Rockefeller mansion stands today. The original mansion burned down in 1902. (See picture, CA:223.) The name is obviously derived from the name of Kykuit Hill. It appears that the name of the Rockefeller estate is a continuation of this tradition.
See Boxwood, Kykuit.
REF: CA:223; M2; M40; ZU:98.

Kidd's Rock
In legend, this rock was where Frederick Philipse I conspired with Captain William Kidd, the notorious pirate. Legend has it that Philipse would light a fire on this rock to beckon Kidd's ship. Philipse owned significant shipping interests and was known to be engaged in smuggling, as were many other Americans of the colonial period. Lord Bellomont, the British colonial governor, suspected that Philipse had obtained and hidden Kidd's contraband "treasures." Kidd was captured, transported to England, and executed in 1701.

According to Jenkins [JE], Kidd and Philipse were closely connected: "He was one of the backers of Captain Kidd in Governor Bellomont's time, and it is stated that Lord Bellomont remarked that: 'If the coffers of Frederick Philipse were searched, Captain Kidd's missing treasures could easily be found.'" Due to Governor Bellomont's accusations, Philipse was ordered removed from the provincial council, but he preempted this order by resigning. Adolph Philipse was also implicated in these smuggling charges, but it appears from his subsequent terms in high public office that this blemish on his reputation did not stick.

Kidd's Rock is located on the river wall near the south end of Kingsland Point Park, not far north of the lighthouse. Ambrose Kingsland had a summerhouse or gazebo built on the rock, which can still be seen in photos as late as 1910. [See a pictures of the rock on pages 13 and 86 of Hutchinson.] Bacon [1898] confirms that a summerhouse was built over the landmark and that the rock had been known as Kidd's Rock for a long time.

Kidd's Rock
And the Tappan Zee, looking north.
Photo by Henry Steiner.

Steel fittings have been driven into the landmark to support a railing which bridges the rock. It seems strange that no one has seen fit to mark or protect Kidd's Rock. The writer has composed a proposal to this end which will soon be submitted to the village and county legislative boards.

REF: BA:25,114;   CON:27-28;   DU:5;   HU:13,[&pic],85,86[pic],184 [pic];   JE:346-347;   LE:77;   M57;   MO:6;   OC: [vol.4]390,395-396,411; RO:np; SH:212-213; ST; TA:12,13; TN [June 21 1996 & pic].

Kingsland Estate, the

The holdings of Ambrose Kingsland (1804-1878) were referred to by this name. Kingsland, a former mayor of New York, owned land in the Tarrytowns in the early 1850s. By the 1870s, his lands extended over most of what is today Philipse Manor, much of Sleepy Hollow Manor, Kingsland Point County Park, and much of the area surrounding the Tarrytown Lakes. Philipse Castle and the Upper Mills were also owned by Kingsland. He built a stone house on Kingsland Point after selling his estate near Sunnyside in 1854. The Kingsland Point house served as a naval training station during World War I.

Kingsland became prosperous working with his brother in the wholesale grocery business. With a fleet of ships, they became leading importers of sperm oil in the years before the petroleum boom. Kingsland also speculated successfully in New York City real estate. He was New York City's last Whig mayor, and he was said to be "an ardent admirer of Henry Clay."

See Kingsland Point and Kingsland Point Park.

REF: HU:85,110,176; JE:381; M37; M40; M41; M65; SC:309[&pic]; TN [Sept. 27 1996 & pic], [June 21 1996 & pic].

Kingsland Point

This was a small peninsula on the north side of the Pocantico River's former mouth. Its shape has been changed due to twentieth century excavation and landfill operations. Today the point does not look much like a point, but the contours of its elevation suggests its former outline. Until the 1920s the outlet of the Pocantico River was where the General Motors Plant stands today. The river was then redirected, and today it enters the Hudson further north, near the gatehouse of the county park.

In 1900, John Brisbane Walker (b. 1847) built a steam automobile factory designed by Sanford White (1853-1906) on the point. Walker was a businessman with eclectic interests who had been intrigued by the Stanley steam car. After a short partnership with Amzi L. Barber, Walker produced steam cars at the Kingsland Point plant from March 1900 until the spring of 1903, when his car company, the Mobile Company, went out of business. The plant and land were then purchased by the Maxwell-Briscoe Motor Company. [See GM.] Later, the site at the mouth of the Pocantico was owned by Chevrolet and finally by General Motors.

An 1864 map clearly identifies Kingsland Point [M62]. Ambrose Kingsland's house stood on the point, and in 1917 it served as a Naval Reserve Base.

See Beekman's Point, Pugsley's Point, Kingsland Estate, Kingsland Point Park.

VAR: *Kingsland's Point.*

REF: *BAC:216; CA:74,233-234; DA2 [Mar. 12 1937], [Feb. 13 1943]; DAI:31; DE:1; GE:13; GM:3,8-10; IN:54,58; M62; M19; M20:26; M40; M42; MO:10,18,25; WEST:[pic. opp. p.728].*

Kingsland Point Park

This is the name of the county park located at Kingsland Point. The park once included De Vries Field, which is currently owned by the Village of Sleepy Hollow. Kingsland Point Park offers picnic areas, Hudson River fishing, a ballfield, playground, and spectacular views of the Hudson's Tappan Zee. Recent budget cuts have curtailed swimming and boating activities there.

The county of Westchester purchased the point from the Village of North Tarrytown in the 1920s. The village re-purchased it in the 1930s, but the county bought it once again in the 1950s.

See Kingsland Point, Pugsley's Point, Beekman Point.

VAR: *Kingsland Point County Park, Kingsland Park.*

REF: *CA:192; HU:154,212,234; M19; M47; M58; MO:30; PE1: vol.24/3 323; SC:309-310; TA:map; DA2 [July 12 1945]; TAR:45.*

Knapp's Corners*

See East Tarrytown, East View.

REF: *CA:316; SC:312.*

Kykuit

According to Piet Wesselman, a Dutch antiquarian bookseller in Amsterdam, the modern spelling of this name is *kijkuit*, meaning lookout. The hill is intersected by the eastern border of the Village of Sleepy Hollow. The summit (474 feet above sea level [TAR]) is the site of the Rockefeller mansion, also called Kykuit. Bacon writes that in the days of the American Revolution beacon fires were lit on this hilltop to warn of British attacks from the south. A number of sources add that it also served, at various times, as an Indian "signal-hill," a lookout, and a "coast survey station."

According to Scharf, the hill was named Kijkuit by the Dutch, but the name was in time corrupted to Kaakout. The Dutch noun *kijk* means view or outlook, and the preposition *uit* means out of, or from. Scharf gives 498 feet as the height of the hill above the Hudson, "next to the highest hill in the county." Lederer [LE] is apparently the only written source to offer the spelling *kijhuit* "peephole," which appears to be an unlikely version. He gives the hill height as 160 meters. In the United States Geological Survey map, its height is indicated as approximately 480 feet.

Legend has it that colonial Dutch residents of the neighborhood were given to reveling on this site. Bacon passes on the story of Rambout Van Dam, an ill-fortuned Dutchman who left a late party at "Kyk-uit," bragging he would row home on the Tappan Zee. He is doomed forever to row through the dense fogs of these waters. In Irving's version of the story, "Kakiat" is located on the west shore of the Hudson. There is also the story of Jacob the Roman, who was said to have made his home on Kykuit in colonial days. See the romantic story of Captain Jacob Romer and his wife Judah in Bacon [BA].

In 1893, John D. Rockefeller bought seventeen or eighteen parcels of land on or near Kykuit Hill, at a cost of $168,705. He continued to purchase contiguous land in the neighborhood. The hilltop became a hub of activity as Rockefeller's workers took down buildings, blasted rock ledge, and removed old fences and walls.

The original wood-frame residence burned down in 1902. It had been owned by a man named Wentworth and was known as the Parsons-Wentworth House. For the next seven years the Rockefeller family lived in the Kent house on the estate. (See M40 for the estate of E. H. Kent and the position of the house on the north side of Bedford Road.)

The twentieth century mansion planned by John D Rockefeller, Jr., and completed in 1913 was named after Kykuit Hill. In 1994, it was opened to public tours operated by Historic Hudson Valley. The estate is still visited by many famous persons; part of the mansion is operated as a conference center.

See Boxwood, Kaakoote, Sugar Loaf Hill, Davids' Hill.

VAR: Kyk-uit, Kyk-Uit, Kijkuit hill, Keakeout Hill, Kaakoote, Kaakiat, Kaakout, Kaa Keoot, Kykuit Hill, Kaakeout, Kijkuit, Kakeout; Kakiat; kijhuit.

REF: BA:117-122,123-125; BI:np; BOL:vol.I,550; CA:13; CAL2; [May 1 1994]; CAS:269,576; CON:11,21,37; DA [Oct. 13 1993], DA2 [May 24 1937], GET:22; HU:26,105,181; IN:53; IR:307-308; LE:79; M17; M19; M28; M40; M41; M57; MA:156,850-851; MO:28; NE [Aug. 21 1994]; NEV:288-289 vol.2; OW:26; SC:305; TAR:6; TN [May 31 1996 & pic]; [May 26 1937]; WES:Vol.32, No. 4; WESS; ZU:98-99.

Lagana Field

This field was occasionally used for ice skating. Located on Sheldon Avenue in Pennybridge, it is frequently used for baseball, AYSO soccer, and other activities today. The field was named for Joe Lagana, who was in charge of Tarrytown's recreation department for many years. The land was once owned by T. C. Eastman [see Millbrook].

REF: CA:173,183; GE:48; LE:79.

Larchlawn

This was the estate of a Colonel Strong. It was located between Hudson Terrace and the First Reformed Church (now the Presbyterian Korean Church of Westchester). An 1881 map of North Tarrytown (the Village of Sleepy Hollow) [M18] shows the land belonging to "Hrs. Col. Strong," or the heirs of Colonel Strong. This may have been the family of Latham Cornell Strong, a popular author of the 1870s.

It appears that the land was subsequently owned by Dr. J. H. Furman. The development of this land was begun by Carl C. Loh and continued in 1924 by James Deeley. At that time the house formerly belonging to Dr. Furman was modified into three apartments.

REF: CA:307; DA2 [Feb. 4 1924]; HU:180;M18; M40.

Lehman Estate
See Elmbrook.
REF: TA:map.

Lemonade Rock
This is the rocky summit of the hill which stands above the cul-de-sac at Crest Drive. The name seems to have been inspired by the feldspar-rich, pink granite exposed on the hilltop. The writer recollects that this hill was occasionally used by neighbors as a private picnic spot in the 1950s. He is not certain whether the name is still in use.
REF: ST.

Lindens, the
This was the nineteenth-century estate of R. E. Hopkins on Broadway, opposite Church Street. Hopkins apparently resided here before moving to Veruselle, a lavish estate just south of Lyndhurst.
See Veruselle.
REF: M40.

Lister's Mill
Hutchinson [HU] suggests that, at one time, there may have been a Philipse mill at this location. Lister and his brother Edwin operated a button and fertilizer factory on the site. Edwin is buried in Sleepy Hollow Cemetery. The mill was sold by Walter Lister in 1868 to Charles Brombacher.

Under Brombacher, the mill powered the Pocantico Tool and Die Works. This was a state of the art factory, operating on water power for ten months of the year and on steam during the summer. Brombacher's residence was located on the east side of the Pocantico, slightly to the south of the mill.

The site of the mill dam is clearly visible today, about two-tenths of a mile upstream from the Sleepy Hollow Cemetery south gate. The pond which formerly stood behind the dam was used for swimming and skating by the residents of the neighborhood.
REF: CA:310; HU:22; SC:304; WES:31:79.

Loh Park
Loh Park is a residential development on the east side of Broadway, opposite Church Street. It was named for Carl C. Loh, an

Orchard Street-based realtor who developed the area.
REF: CA:206,269; DA2 [June 13 1942], [Feb. 20 1943]; TA:map; TAR:40.

Long View

Long View was the name of the Douglas estate on Prospect Hill. According to Hutchinson [HU], the house had an observatory with views of the countryside. Scharf [SC] describes it as the "country-seat of Henry L. Douglas."

See Prospect Hill, Douglas Estate, Douglas Park.
REF: HU:176,178[pic]; SC:306.

Losee Park

This is a Village of Tarrytown recreational park, located between the Tarrytown Boat Club and the Washington Irving Boat Club. One source records that the park was established in 1965. It includes a picnic area, playground, and two ballfields known as Basher Park.

According to Lederer [LE], the park was established in 1972, and it was named for James Losee, Tarrytown's former village engineer. A picture of Losee (b.1888) appears in TARR with a brief profile. He was superintendent of Tarrytown's water department for over thirty years. He also served as a village trustee and as a consultant to the village on engineering matters. In August of 1945, Losee served on a committee which traveled to Albany to seek Hudson River land grants for Tarrytown. Losee was responsible for compiling information connected with Tarrytown's plans for harbor improvements, recreational facilities, an access road on the west side of the railroad tracks, a bus station, and a parking area.

VAR: Loosee Park (a typographic error from the NY Times).
REF: CA:183; DA2 [Aug. 11 1945]; DAI:36; GE:48; LE:85; M20:22. M58; NE [Aug. 21 1994]; TARR:np [& pic].

Lower Crest, the

The Lower Crest is that part of the Crest (or Tarry Crest) located near Benedict Avenue.

See the Tarry Crest.
REF: ST.

Lower Crossroads

This road has been confused with Route 119. It is actually Route 100C, stretching past the Hammond House, the ancient "Four Corners," the Westchester County Medical Center, and Westchester Community College. To add to the confusion over this place name, Raymond refers to this road as "the upper road from Tarrytown," or "the County House road."

The Upper Crossroads and Lower Crossroads were also the names of Mount Pleasant hamlets in the mid-nineteenth century.

See Youngs Corners and County House Road.

VAR: *Lower Crossroad, the County House Road, the County House road.*
REF: *HUT:17,85; LE:85; M39; RA:197; RAY:11; SC:312; SH:591; WE:205.*

Lower Lake, the

This is the larger of the two Tarrytown Lakes, the one closer to East View. The two lakes are separated by a causeway. It should be noted that Lederer [LE] refers to another lake, near Tarrytown's southern boarder, as the Lower Lake.

VAR: *Lower Reservoir.*
REF: *LE:85; M20:23; M45; M47; M49; M58; TAR:22.*

Luke Estate

The former Goebel Collector's Club showroom on Route 119 was once the Luke mansion. The Luke Estate lay north of Route 119, both east and west of Broadway. The house was originally built by Judge Martin Rumsey Miller in 1905. Miller bought the estate from George B. Newton, whose house had burned in 1904. Subsequently, Thomas Luke brought the property in 1909. Luke was an owner of West Virginia Pulp and Paper Company. The *Tarrytown Daily News* of January 26, 1937, mentions that Miss Janet Luke of 105 While Plains Road was the chairperson of a drive to help flood victims. In the twentieth century, the estate has also been owned by Simmonds Laboratories.

In October of 1996, the Marshall Cavendish Corporation, a publisher of reference and educational books, moved its headquarters to the building. Times Publishing Limited is the parent company of Marshall Cavendish Corporation. The property had been purchased in 1994 and the building renovated. The structure is now set on five acres of land.

REF: *DA2 [Jan. 26 1937]; GE:30; TA:map; TAP:np; TN [Oct. 18 1996]; ZU:81.*

Lyndhurst

Lyndhurst means "forest of Linden trees." In the early nineteenth century, this property was owned by William Paulding, Jr. He was the brother of James K. Paulding, an early literary collaborator of Washington Irving, and later, the Secretary of the United States Navy. William Paulding had been a New York City mayor and a congressman, and he called his property "Knoll." [See LYN.] The house was designed for him in the late 1830s by Alexander Jackson Davis (1803-1892), a noted architect. The building was later expanded by Davis for a second owner, George Merritt, who also built the first greenhouse. It was Merritt who named the estate Lyndhurst.

Jay Gould (1836-1892), a railroad tycoon, bought the estate in 1880, seven years after Merritt's death. By 1886, he owned a seventy-five acre parcel west of Broadway and a parcel of 625 acres east of Broadway. Gould had control of several railroads and Western Union, as well as many other business interests. His reputation as a "robber-baron" made him widely disliked.

In the early twentieth century Lyndhurst belonged to Gould's daughter, Helen (d. 1938). Helen was married to Finley J. Shepard (1867-1942). She was an active philanthropist who, for a time, opened her estate to convalescent soldiers after the Spanish-American War. Mrs. Shepard also founded Lyndhurst Clubhouse on Sheldon Avenue, opposite the old Pennybridge School. This was a recreation facility for girls and boys. Later, her sister Anna Gould (d. 1961), the Duchess of Talleyrand, relocated here from Europe at the advent of the Second World War. The sixty-seven-acre estate then passed into the hands of the National Trust for Historic Preservation, which hosts approximately 100,000 visitors per year at the site.

See Paulding Manor.

VAR: *Lyndenhurst (Lynden Forest), Lyndehurst, Knoll.*
REF: *BAC:231; BI:np; BOL:vol.I,292,293; CAL1; CAL2; CON:23; DA2 [Aug. 5 1942]; GE:12,25,26; GET:21; IN:51; KE:230[pic]; LYN:np; M29; M40; MI:15[cap]; NE [Aug. 21 1994]; TN [May 31 1996]; WES:Vol.34:19; ZU:83-85; SC:243.*

Malkasten

The estate of artist Albert Bierstadt was called Malkasten. The name, meaning "music box," was inspired by an artists' club in Dusseldorf, Germany. The artist originally named the place Hawksrest. Neighborhood friend John C. Frémont was a patron of Bierstadt's work.

The artist first bought 5.65 acres of land south of Lyndhurst and east of Broadway in 1865. He continued to add to this initial purchase over several years. The house, a grand residence designed in 1866, stood west of Broadway between Lyndhurst and Wolfert's Dell. It burned down in 1882.

REF: *AND:34,35; WES [Fall 1991, p. 77-79]; ZU:87.*

Maplehurst

Maplehurst appears on a map of 1926. It was the estate of Robert Hoe, Jr. (d. 1909), and it lay just south of Cedar Cliff. Hoe's firm was the first to manufacture the rotary printing press. The estate had an area of twenty-four acres and lay to the north of Van Wart Avenue, where today the Tappan Zee Bridge meets the Tarrytown shore. Hoe was interested in the raising of cattle, so his estate boasted an impressive menagerie; there was also a large greenhouse on the estate. He is buried at Sleepy Hollow Cemetery.

One source [SC] reports that the William Hunt farmhouse formerly stood on the site of Hoe's house. The farm was purchased by Hunt from the New York State Commissioners of Forfeiture in 1785. He held 270 acres of land, which bordered the Hudson between Paulding Avenue and Martling Avenue and extended eastward to include all of Glenville. The Hunt farm encompassed all or part of Crest Lawn, Braemar, and Barron Court, among other parcels and estates.

REF: *CA:235,310; M29; M38; M40; SC:232; TA:29-30; TWO:56.*

Maple Terrace

In 1871 this estate on White Plains Road was owned by James H. Benedict. He may have been a relation of General James Benedict, who purchased the Benedict estate in 1826.

See Barron Court.

REF: *M56.*

Marschke's Grove

Canning and Buxton [CA] describe this chestnut grove in Pennybridge; the exact location is not specified. The American chestnut trees were destroyed by a blight early in this century. Who Marschke was is not clear, but it may be worth noting that on September 15, 1914, E. Marschke of Sheldon Avenue was in Tarrytown when his barn caught fire and burned. See the *Tarrytown Daily News* article [DA]. "The barn was near the large ice houses owned by Clarence Brown." In addition, the name John Marschke appears in a list of Tarrytown fire chiefs for 1940. The family name is still found in the Tarrytown-Irvington area.
REF: CA: 336;239; DA [Sept. 15 1914, p.1].

Marsh Field, the

The name refers to a field once located near the west end of Continental Street. In 1929, Jackson's Lot, a popular recreational spot, was closed due to the construction of the Van Tassel Apartments. At that point the Marsh presented itself as a substitute. It was a area at the foot of Continental Street used as a village dump. An article in the *Tarrytown Daily News* of May 2, 1932, indicates that boys had already been playing ball at the site and that plans were afoot to have the county do some dredging, filling, and leveling there. It appears that shortly after this date, the land was deeded back to the village.

The Marsh Field, not to be confused with De Vries Field, had by the 1950s become a well-developed recreational facility. During the fifties it was dedicated as Donohue Field, but it continued to be known as the Marsh Field. Upon the merging of the North Tarrytown and Tarrytown school systems, the land was sold to General Motors, which constructed a parking lot on the site.

See the recollections of Patrick Munroe and Joseph A. Demilia, Sr., regarding the Marsh in a *Tarry News* [TN] article.

See Donohue Field.
VAR: *The Marsh, the marsh.*
REF: CEC; DA2 [May 21 1932]; M34; SM; ST; TN [Aug. 23 1996], [Aug. 30 1996], [Aug. 16 1996].

Martling's Landing

This landing was named for the Martling family who operated it.

Requa's Dock was subsequently built on this site at the Tarrytown waterfront. In present day terms it was near the Tarrytown police station. Martling's Landing was active in the early days when Tarrytown Bay came right up to lower Franklin Street. In *An Account of The Action at Tarrytown* [AC], the old Martling-Requa Landing was said to be not far from where the Action at Tarrytown took place. This event was a minor Revolutionary War engagement involving American, French, and British forces.

According to *The Old Dutch Burying Ground of Sleepy Hollow* [HIS], Martling's Landing was owned by Captain Daniel Martling who died in 1788, during his fifty-first year. Martling served as a lieutenant in Dutcher's company during the Revolution. He, together with other family members, operated the Tarrytown landing at the foot of White Street, subsequently known as Requa's Dock.

In addition to the Action at Tarrytown, there was another Revolutionary War engagement in the waters off Tarrytown. Daniel Martling's brother, Abraham (d. 6/16/1786) was wounded in the galley naval fight of August 2, 1776, when American galleys attacked two British frigates in the Tappan Zee.

The name Martling's Landing also applied to a landing near the foot of Beekman Avenue. We find it in an advertisement for the sale of "Beekman Farm" quoted in Bacon [BA], December 1822. "Martling and Van Wart's landing" is said to be at the end of the "Public Market Road," the northern boundary of the land advertised for sale. It appears that the Martling family operated both landings at one time. Dorland's map (a modern reconstruction of post-Revolutionary times) [M57], shows Martling's Dock at the foot of Continental Road.

See also an interesting discussion in Duboc [DU] regarding the mode and importance of the Dutch sloop, or riverboat, traffic. Duboc asserts that Nyack enjoyed an ascendancy over the Tarrytowns as a Hudson River port-of-call. This was said to be for navigational reasons having to do with the Hudson River bottom.

See Requa-Martling Dock.

VAR: *Martling Landing, Martlings and Van Wart's landing, old Martling-Requa Dock.*

REF: *AC:9; BA:137,138; CA:36; DU:5-8; HIS:18-19; M22; M57; RA:182; RAY:16.*

Mead-Requa farm, the

According to Raymond [RA], this was a nineteenth century farm in Sleepy Hollow. A map of the late 1860s [M35] shows the Mead place near the juncture of the Pocantico and that tributary known today as Rockefeller Brook.
REF: M35; RA:57.

Mekeel Brook

See Abram Storm Brook.
REF: AR [Apr.1 1882].

Middletown

In 1851 or before, a very small hamlet near Broadway and Benedict Avenue was called Middletown. At the time of the separation of the First Reformed Church and the Second Reformed Church, lands about Church Street were deeded to the latter. Subsequently the property was laid out for dwellings, and this area became known as Middletown. A map dated 1864 [M62] includes this place name. It appears that after the incorporation of the Village of Tarrytown this place name faded from use.
VAR: Middleton.
REF: An 1851 map in the collection of Historic Hudson Valley; HUT:67(map); LE:92; M62; SC:232.

Mile 28

At first sight the damaged, ancient stone marker which stands before the south gate of Sleepy Hollow Cemetery appears to mark a place twenty-eight miles from New York. However it is probable that the marker is in the wrong place. Originally Albany Post Road milestones were placed on the west side of the road. If this is indeed correct, then all remaining east side milestones have been moved to their locations from elsewhere. Many of the original milestones have vanished from the old Post Road over the years. It seems that Milestone 28 was repositioned near the Old Dutch Church of Sleepy Hollow, possibly for safekeeping. According to reliable maps of the Revolutionary period, its original position was near the southern border of Tarrytown (on the west side of the road).

See Mile 32 for an important related discussion.
REF: HU:Title page [pic]; M33; M12; OW:1; RO:22.

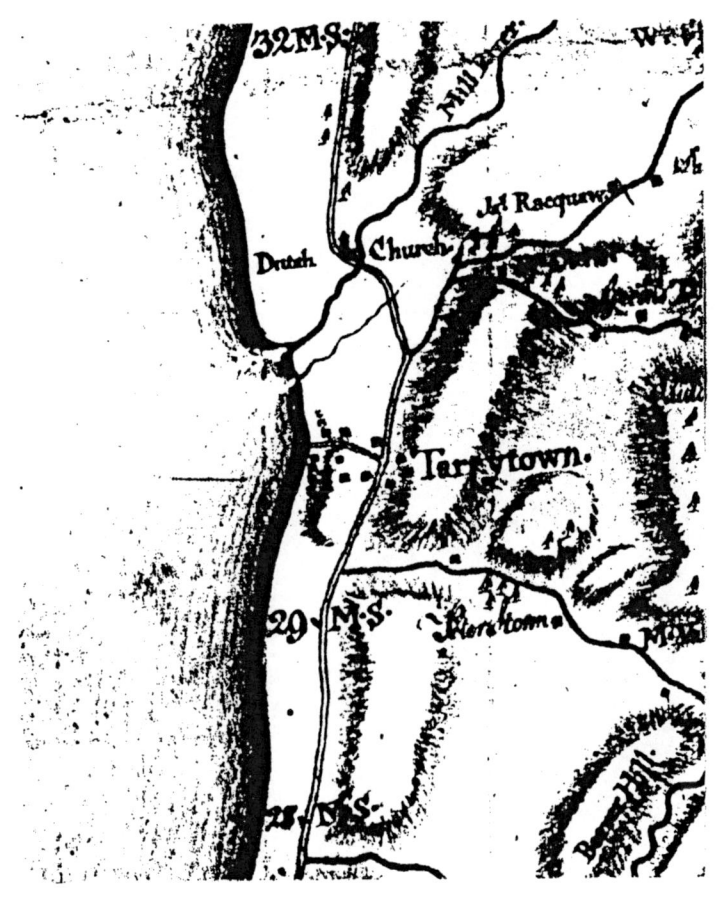

Erskine Compilation Map
Detail [M11] showing Tarrytown & Sleepy Hollow area in the period of the Revolution. Courtesy New York Historical Society.

Mile 32

On October 17, 1851, Captain John Romer stated that, "The old 29 [or 26] milestone, during the Revolutionary War, stood a mile south of Tarrytown." His observation predates the incorporation of the village, so he was referring to the hamlet of Tarrytown rather than southern border of the modern, incorporated village.

According to a history of Irvington [WO], Milestone 32 and other milestones marking the old Albany Post Road were authorized by Benjamin Franklin in his role as Postmaster General of the American Colonies. This local history makes note of the locations of two surviving markers on the west side of Broadway below Tarrytown: Mile 26 in southern Irvington and Mile 27 near Conklin's Tavern on South Broadway in Irvington. (Conklin's Tavern has also been known as the Jan Harmse house or the old Odell Inn.)

Mile 28 would have been near the south border of Tarrytown, Mile 29 near the Tappan Zee Bridge entrance, Mile 30 near Central Avenue in Tarrytown, Mile 31 near the Old Dutch Church, and Mile 32 near Oak Court in Sleepy Hollow Manor.

Maps of the Revolutionary period seem to agree with this picture. Robert Erskine's survey of the road from Tarrytown to the Croton River, dating from 1778 [M12], shows Mile 32 located one mile north of the Old Dutch Church. The Colles map of the Tarrytown area in the same period [COL] is also in agreement. As indicated in the discussion concerning Mile 28, it appears that the twenty-eighth milestone was at some recent time moved to its current location near the Old Dutch Church, perhaps for safekeeping. The stone's original position seems to have been one or two tenths of mile north of Sunnyside Lane.

Today, a check by odometer shows that the relationship of local post-Revolutionary milestone sites have not changed much. The course of the Post Road is very similar to what is was in those early days. Starting from Mile 26 near Mercy College and proceeding north, the only notable discrepancy is between Mile 30 and Mile 31. This can be reconciled by deducting approximately one hundred yards for the Revolutionary period "S curve" at the Pocantico crossing. The Post Road at this crossing is now more direct than it was in the late eighteenth century.

See Mile 28.

REF: *M12; M33; MA:1062; WO:12-13.*

Millbrook

Timothy Corser Eastman (1821-1893) owned Millbrook, a seventy-five-acre estate lying north of Pinkstone and west of Broadway. Eastman was a New Hampshire-born self-made man, a pioneer in the transportation of beef cattle via ship and rail. At one time he was in charge of all New York Central Railroad cattle shipments. He shipped large amounts of live cattle and dressed beef to England and Scotland. [See Dictionary of American Biography Vol. III, page 603.] Eastman was living in Tarrytown at the time of his death.

Eastman acquired his estate some time after the closing of the Institute for the Instruction of the Deaf and Dumb in 1883. He also owned some land east of the aqueduct and north of Sheldon Brook. Mill Brook was named for the mills that operated on Sheldon Brook which passes through the property. Today Kraft General Foods occupies the site.

See Croydon, Sheldon Brook, Pennybridge, the Old Van Weert Mill.
REF: CA:236; M40.

Mill Brook [the Pocantico River]
See Mill River.
REF: M55.

Mill Brook [Sheldon Brook]
This was formerly the name of Sheldon Brook. A mill was in operation there in early times.
See Sheldon Brook and old Van Weert mill.
REF: CA:118,238; LE:92; M40.

Mill Pond, the
Today in the Tarrytowns, when one speaks of the mill pond, one is generally referring to the pond at Philipsburg Manor Restoration. The pond was certainly in existence by the late seventeenth century, although the Philipse dam may well have been preceded by an earlier dam. It has been suggested that the late seventeenth century Philipse Mill was not the first mill on this site.
REF: IRVING:5; M42; M65; ST.

Mill Point

Mill Point is now known as Kingsland Point.
See Beekman Point, Pugsley's Point, Kingsland Point.
REF: *M6; M32; M54; SC:309.*

Mill River

In the eighteenth and nineteenth centuries, this was an alternate name for the Pocantico River. In addition to the original Philipse mill, there were several mills and factories along the river in the nineteenth century. Some suggest there may even have been a mill predating the one built by Philipse in the 1680s.
VAR: *Upper Mill River, Mill river.*
REF: *BO:316,327; BOL:vol.I,505,531; CA:200; M15; M50; M32; OW:6; P2; TN [Nov. 2 1995 & pic]; WES:Vol.12,No.4,p.85.*

Mill Woods, the

The Mill Woods was an alternate name for Beekman Forest.
See Beekman Forest.
REF: *CA:200.*

Miller Park

This residential area was also known as Benedict Park. It was named after John and Samuel Miller who developed it in 1924. The land was previously part of the Benedict estate and, later, Cobb's Lot.
See Benedict estate, Benedict Park and Cobb's Lot.
REF: *CA:204; TA:map; TAR:40; TARR:np.*

Montrose

In the nineteenth century this estate lay on the east side of Broadway, south of the Gould holdings.
REF: *M40.*

Mount André

The hill above the Captors' Monument was known by this name at the time of the 1880 centennial celebration of André's capture. The name also applied to the estate of E. Coles at the top of Cobb Lane in 1871. Earlier the Coles estate was owned by J. Swift.
REF: *HU:121; M17; M38; M56; YE:np.*

Mount Hope

This is the estate of Jacob Storm; in 1871 it lay north of Mekeel Avenue and east of Beech Lane. The estate included all of Suncliff and other lands which Storm had purchased from his father-in-law, Caleb Wildey.

See Suncliff and Wilson Park.

REF: M38; M56.

Mount Pleasant, the Town of

A Westchester County township, the Town of Mount Pleasant was established by New York State on March 7, 1788. The town is twenty-eight miles square and comprises all of the former Manor of Philipsburgh lands north of Greenburgh. The Village of Sleepy Hollow is located in the southwest corner of this township.

See more in Scharf [SC] about Mount Pleasant.

REF: BI:np; HUFE:132-143; M61; M28; M49; M59; SC:282-285; TAR:7; YE:np.

Mount View

In 1871 and earlier, the estate of James Shaw was located west of today's Marymount Avenue, near its north end.

REF: M38; M56.

Nepperhan, the*

This is the Algonquian name for the Saw Mill River which, according to Bolton [BOL], means "fast running water." In "Wolfert's Roost," Irving notes that "The Neperan, [is] vulgarly called the Saw Mill River...."

See Saw Mill River.

VAR: The Nepperhan River, Neppiran, Nippizan, Nippiorha, Neperan, Nepera.

REF: BA:81; BOL:vol.I,268; BOL:vol:II,576,592-593; HIN:267; IR:302; LE:100; PHILI:19; TA:9,10; YE:np; WO:10.

Nest, the

This was formerly the home of C. Graham, located in the southwest corner of Martling Avenue.

REF: M40.

Neutral Ground, the

During the Revolution, much of Westchester County, including the area of the Tarrytowns, was known as the Neutral Ground, a hotly contested, war-ravaged terrain. Fighting often pitted neighbor against neighbor and sometimes brother against brother. The Neutral Ground was far from being a haven of neutrality; it was more accurately a no man's land. Farms were stripped bare by the partisans of both sides in the conflict, and whole communities were uprooted.

British forces, and the American Loyalist troopers who cooperated with them, occupied New York and that portion of southern Westchester now known as the Bronx. The local American Revolutionary forces had garrisons near the Croton River and Peekskill. Both sides frequently launched strikes against each other through Westchester County. In addition, due to their foraging activities in this area, local inhabitants were frequently picked clean. Even more devastating and frightening were the parties of unauthorized freebooters who preyed on the homesteaders. The Cowboys (Loyalist partisans) and the Skinners (American Revolutionary partisans) were widely feared by friend and foe alike. These groups patrolled the countryside, settling old scores and depriving the inhabitants of the very means of subsistence. The character of the fighting in Westchester County was as much that of a civil war as it was a war for independence.

Note: See a new interpretation of the term, Skinners, in Lincoln Diamant's, *Yankee Doodle Days*.

VAR: neutral ground, neutral territory, No Man's Land.
REF: BACO:8; BOL:vol.II,p.612; CON:29; CRA:30; DA2 [Mar. 12 1937]; DE:5; GE:11; HAD2:1-5; HIN:268; HUFE:72; LE:100; LOS:185-186; OE:30; PHI:np; TA:17; TAR:2; VAND:340; WE:200,201,203; WI:144; YE:np.

New Croton Aqueduct, the

The construction of this aqueduct meant a business boom for the Rand Drill Works, the manufacturers of the Rand Percussion Rock Drill, located in the Village of North Tarrytown (Sleepy Hollow). Construction began in 1885, after severe regional droughts put excessive demand on the Old Croton Aqueduct. The New Aqueduct passes by the Tarrytown Lakes.
REF: CRO:5; SC:305; TAR:27.

North Landing

This was a name for the landing at the foot of Beekman Avenue in the years after the Civil War. It was one of the three main landings in the two villages. Canning [CA] adds that "many vessels were built at the North Landing with timber cut in the dense forests of the Mill Woods (Beekman's forest)...."

See Steamboat Landing and South Landing. See especially Beekmantown Landing.

REF: CA:63,200.

North River

"North River" was the name commonly applied to the Hudson in Revolutionary days. Van der Donck used the term more than one hundred years earlier (in a Dutch form, of course) in his prospectus on the New Netherlands. Early colonists considered the Hudson to be the North River and the Delaware to be the South River.

See Hudson River.

REF: AC:11,15; BOL:vol.I,268; HIST:179; LE:103; M16; TWO:64; VA:10.

North Tarrytown, the Village of [the Village of Sleepy Hollow]

This name may have been invented by postal authorities when they opened a Beekmantown post office in 1871. Others sources suggest that, due to the incorporation of the Village of Tarrytown in 1870, local residents began to differentiate the small center to the north as North Tarrytown. A political handbill of 1873, promoting incorporation, invited voters to the post office for a meeting on the subject.

The initials NT were employed as a popular short form, or nickname. On occasion, portions of North Tarrytown were referred to as "Tarrytown." This convention seems to have been a throwback to pre-incorporation times when portions of the village were loosely referred to as Tarrytown. [See Tarrytown, Village of.]

Two large areas of the village had their own place names before North Tarrytown's incorporation, Sleepy Hollow and Beekmantown.

See Village of Sleepy Hollow, Sleepy Hollow, Beekmantown.

VAR: *North Tarrytown, N. T., NT, the upper Tarrytown.*
REF: GM:3; GR:48; HU:2,102-106; I1; LE:103; M28; M43; M49; M58; MI:1; MO3; NOR:np; NORT:3; RO:5; SH:611,619; TAR:2; WO:9.

Old Croton Aqueduct
Viewed from the top of the Pocantico River viaduct. Photo by Henry Steiner.

Northcote

Northcote was the nine-and-a-half-acre estate of Mrs. H. R. Worthington, located opposite Wolfert's Dell. It stood somewhat to the south of Lyndhurst between Broadway and the Croton Aqueduct. Benson Ferris built a house here in 1835, after selling Wolfert's Roost to Washington Irving. His estate was called the Homestead in Scharf [SC].

According to the *Tarrytown Argus*, Henry R. Worthington was "extensively engaged in the manufacture of pumps" and had lived in "Irvington" for 20 years at the time of his death in 1880. For part of the Worthingtons' tenure, the estate was considered to be in Irvington, but the incorporation of Tarrytown in 1870 placed it, along with Sunnyside, within the borders of the Village of Tarrytown.

See the Homestead.
REF: AR [Dec. 18 1880]; M40; SC:242; TA:29.

Northern Depot

This was formerly a train station on the Putnam line. It was located in Tarrytown Heights at the intersection of Sunnyside Avenue and Neperan Road.
VAR: *Northern Rail Depot.*
REF: CA:136,193,198,314.

Northern Tarrytown*

In 1900, Miller [MI] gives this name as the birth place of Admiral John L. Warden, commander of the Civil War ironclad, the *Monitor*. Warden was born in Scarborough.
REF: MI:20.

Old Croton Aqueduct, the

The Old Croton Aqueduct was the first aqueduct to carry water to New York City. It roughly paralleled the Hudson River along its course. Finished in 1842, its construction must have caused a great stir in this community. The aqueduct is said to have delivered approximately 100,000,000 gallons per day. The route of Broadway as it passed through the Tarrytowns is thought to have been changed in several places at the time of the aqueduct's construction.

When the viaduct crossing of the Pocantico was being built, Washington Irving enjoyed watching its progress. George Law,

Old Dutch Burying Ground
Headstone depicting an angel or the soul of the departed. Photo by Henry Steiner.

another local resident, was the contractor of this project. George S. Rice's land touched the eastern end of the viaduct.

See Croton Aqueduct.

VAR: *first Croton Aqueduct.*
REF: *CRO:1-15; HUFE:249-250,252; IN:48; M5; M58; SC:307; TAR:4; TN [Oct. 31 1996]; TW:23.*

Old Dutch Burying Ground

This name applies strictly to the small graveyard surrounding the Old Dutch Church of Sleepy Hollow; it does not apply to Sleepy Hollow Cemetery. According to *The Old Dutch Burying Ground of Sleepy Hollow*, interments are believed to predate 1650. At the turn of the eighteenth century, there were said to have been 180 graves.

This land was set aside by Frederick Philipse I when he had the church built in the late seventeenth century. In the time of the Revolution, when all the lands of Frederick Philipse III were confiscated by the State of New York, the churchyard was included; however, it was soon deeded back to the congregation.

Today the Old Dutch Burying Ground is regularly open for tours. The use of power mowers and trimmers has accelerated the deterioration of the stones the twentieth century. The effects of acid rain has also been destructive. The caretakers of the burying ground invite visitors to photograph the stones, but the taking of rubbings is prohibited.

Washington Irving wrote in his reminiscence titled, "Sleepy Hollow":

> Let me speak of this quiet grave-yard with all due reverence, for I owe it amends for the heedlessness of my boyish days. I blush to acknowledge the thoughtless frolic with which, in company with whipsters, I have sported within its sacred bounds during intervals of worship; chasing butterflies, plucking wild flowers, or vieing with each other who could leap over the tallest tomb-stones; until checked by the stern voice of the sexton.

It is certain that any modern-day leapfrogging would be "checked by the stern voice of the sexton" as well. See a *Tarry News* article [TN Nov. 22, 1995] for comments on the erosion of

Old Dutch Church of Sleepy Hollow
Erected by Frederick Philipse I circa 1685. Photo by Henry Steiner.

gravestones.
VAR: Old Dutch Church and Burying Ground, Old Dutch Churchyard, old Dutch Churchyard, Old Church Yard, Old Dutch Graveyard, Old Dutch Burial Ground, Old Dutch Burying Ground of Sleepy Hollow, Old Dutch Church and Grave Yard, Old Dutch Church burial ground; Sleepy Hollow church-yard.
REF: AN2:np; CA:309 ; COLL:title page; DA2 [Oct. 27 1933 pic]; GE:12,27; HIS:7; HU:26,96,200; IR:309; IRVIN:108; LOS:187; M21; M34; M50; M57; M65; OW:13,21; P3; RA:79; TAR:2; TN [July 19 1996], [May 17 1996 & pic], [Nov. 22 1995 & pic]; TWO:8; WIL:[pic].

Old Dutch Church, the

The Old Dutch Church of Sleepy Hollow is the oldest church building in New York State. It is one of the oldest American churches (perhaps the oldest) still used as a house of worship. The "Old Dutch" was designated a National Historic Landmark in 1963.

Washington Irving's well-known description of the church appears in the "The Legend of Sleepy Hollow":

> The sequestered situation of this church seems always to have made it a favorite haunt of troubled spirits. It stands on a knoll, surrounded by locust-trees and lofty elms, from among which its decent whitewashed walls shine modestly forth, like Christian purity beaming through the shades of retirement. A gentle slope descends from it to a silver sheet of water, bordered by high trees, between which, peeps may be caught at the blue hills of the Hudson. To look upon its grass-grown yard, where the sunbeams seem to sleep so quietly, one would think that there at least the dead might rest in peace.

Frederick Philipse I had the church built about 1685, when it was no doubt intended to help attract new tenants to Philipsburgh Manor. The VF on the weather vane stands for Vedryck Flypsen, an archaic spelling of the name of Frederick Philipse I.

It is a common modern scholarly prejudice to assume that details of old paintings depicting the Sleepy Hollow landscape are full of inaccuracies and fanciful elements, particularly when they include something unexpected. Author John K. Howat [HO] comments on one old painting of the Old Dutch Church, "In this case, the artist has enriched the composition with the addition of the columned portico on the oldest church in New York State...." It is actually Howat who does the "enriching." He apparently was unaware that the church *did* have a portico for a time during the nineteenth century. This can be easily verified from records of the church in that period and by examining other period paintings. The portico is said to have adorned the church between 1837 and 1857. Major repairs were made to the church in 1837 when it partially burned after a lightening strike [RO:23].

The portico had been removed when Lossing [LO] and Currier produced renderings of the church some time between 1860 and 1866, but it can be seen in an undated painting [HO] and an etching in *Gleason's Pictorial* [P3, January 8, 1853]. Restoration work to the roof and belfry of the structure was conducted in 1990.

It is possible to observe the progressive growth of certain neighboring trees by carefully comparing the many renderings of the Old Dutch Church, Philipse Castle, and the Headless Horseman Bridge. These clues, as well as the evidence on prominent gravestones, can be helpful in dating some of the undated Sleepy Hollow landscape paintings of the nineteenth century.

VAR: *old Dutch Church, Old Dutch Church of Sleepy Hollow, old Dutch Church of Sleepy Hollow, old Sleepy Hollow Dutch Church, Old Sleepy Hollow Church, Sleepy Hollow Church, Old Dutch Church at Sleepy Hollow, Old Dutch Church in Sleepy Hollow, the Old Dutch, the Philipsburgh church, The Dutch Church of the Manor of Phillipsburgh, The Church of Philipsburgh, the Dutch Reformed Church of Sleepy Hollow, the Dutch Reformed Church in Sleepy Hollow, the Manor Church of Philipsburgh, the Old Dutch Church of Philipsburgh, the First Reformed Church of Tarrytown, the church at Tarrytown, The Old Church of Sleepy Hollow.*

REF: *AN:57; AN2:np; CA:309; COLL:4,7; DA2 [Dec. 7 1929]; DAI:31; DE:7; ; GE:12,27; GET:28; GM:6 & pic; HA:102-108; HARP:np[pic]; HIS:10; HISTOR:np; HUFE:132; IR:309; LO:320,321; LOS:190[&pic]; MA:172; M57; M32; M42; MO:33; P3; P8; PE1: vol.24/3 323,326,343; PHI:np; RAYM:np; SH:505,163; SL:np; TA:11-12; TA2:np; TAP:np; TAR:2; TARR:np; TN [Dec. 13 1996], [Apr. 26 1996 & pic]; TW:3,6,27; TWO:5-7,52,82,83,111,157;   WES:Vol.12,No.4,p.85,95,97;   WIL:pic]; YE:np.*

Old Mill of Sleepy Hollow
   This name is sometimes applied to the mill built by Frederick Philipse at the Upper Mills, and sometimes to Carl's Mill.
   See Carl's Mill.
VAR: the Old Mill.
REF: DA2 [Apr. 16 1942], [Jan. 25 1943]; PHI:np; RO:np.

Old Redoubt, the
   See Battle Hill.
REF: RA:36.

Old Van Weert Mill, the
   The Van Weert family formerly owned two mills on Sheldon Brook. Gerrit Van Weert was a deacon of the Old Dutch Church in 1697. The farm of 240 acres appears to have passed from Gerrit (who lived on this land by 1698) to his son Jan. Later his grandson Isaac owned the land. Isaac is not to be confused with one of the captors of Major André by the same name. Isaac sold some of the property to Henry Sheldon, who built his home at the mill site.
   According to Scharf [SC], the mill became useless after the flow of Sheldon Brook abated. Scharf seems unaware that there had been more than one Van Weert mill. The William Adams map of Greenburgh [M31] (c. 1797) shows the two mills within one hundred yards of the Hudson. They both stood on the south side of the brook, with the saw mill positioned slightly upstream of the grist mill. Which of these was referred to in the late nineteenth-century Scharf account is unclear. Sheldon sold the property to a banker named William Hoge (d. 1875), who was forced to give the place up after having financial difficulties. In 1879, the site was acquired by the Institution for the Instruction of the Deaf and Dumb. The school removed from the site in 1883. Subsequently, Timothy C. Eastman purchased the estate and named it Millbrook. By the 1920s the estate appears on a local map as Croydon.
   See Sheldon Brook, Croydon, Millbrook, Old Van Weert Mill.
REF: BOL:vol.I,293; FI:9; M1; M33; SC:231,244.

Over back
   This vague-sounding term was used by early inhabitants of Tarrytown to refer to the area of the Tarrytown Lakes and Eastview.

REF: SC:194.

Patriots Park

Named for the three Americans who captured Major John André, this park straddles André's Brook on the border of the two villages. The young patriots were John Paulding, David Williams, and Isaac Van Wart. Patriots Park extends from Broadway to Washington Street, and from the Warner Library to College Avenue. The area of the park was home to Highland Manor School in the first half of the twentieth century. Lauren Bacall attended the school as a girl during the 1930s [*Vanity Fair*, Feb. 1997, see picture].

According to Florence Kane, director of the Warner Library, the park was named Patriots Park by Cornelia Blakemore Warner (1859-1947), wife of Worcester R. Warner (1846-1929). The Warners paid for the building of the Warner Library and the surrounding property.

Hutchinson [HU] notes that the land of Patriots Park was purchased by Mrs. Worcester R. Warner and Mrs. Victor Spanberg and then given to the villages of Tarrytown and North Tarrytown during the 1940s. At a later date, Tarrytown purchased North Tarrytown's (Sleepy Hollow's) portion of the park.

The park includes a small playground and basketball court. A small circular drive connects several handsome stone bridges.

See André Brook, Captors' Monument, Brookside Park, Wildey's Swamp.

VAR: *Patriot's Park, Patriots' Park.*
REF: *DA2: [Feb. 23 1929]; DAI:31,36; GE:11,48; GET:29; HU:227,232; KA; LE:107; M45; M58.*

Paulding Manor

This is one of the names by which Lyndhurst was known during the tenure of its original owner, William Paulding, Jr. Paulding was the nephew of John Paulding, one of the captors of Major André. He was also the brother of James K. Paulding, a United States Secretary of the Navy and literary collaborator of Washington Irving. William Paulding, Jr., a lawyer, was serving as mayor of New York City (1824-1826, 1827-1829) when Lafayette visited the city.

According to Lossing [LO] and Scharf [SC], the house was built in 1840. A recent article in the *Tarry News* [TN] gives the construction date of 1838 and credits Andrew Jackson Davis with the

Paulding Manor
Later known as Lynhurst. Etching by Lossing.

design. By 1846, the property was transferred to Philip R. Paulding, Esq., and in 1864 it was sold to George Merritt. Merritt had sold his nearby residence to Robert Hoe (See Maplehurst). It was Merritt who named the place Lyndhurst; Jay Gould purchased the estate in 1880.

Note that Butler [BU] appears to confuse Paulding Manor with the home of William Paulding's father, also named William. That house was located near Martling's Landing.

See Lyndhurst.
VAR: *The Paulding Place, Paulding's folly.*
REF: *BU:32; CA:224; IN:51; LO:340-341; M60; TA:29; TARR:np; TN [May 31 1996]; WES:Vol.34:19.*

Peabody Field

Located just north of Philipse Manor, Peabody Field is owned by the School District of the Tarrytowns. It was formerly part of the Webb estate. Webb sold the land to George Peabody, who was noted for his generosity. At least a portion of the Peabody lands were owned by the Peabody Clay Company. The land was left to the school system by Mrs. Peabody.

According to Hutchinson [HU], the field was once the site of a Girl Scout camp. Today the field is used for soccer matches, neighborhood events, and other activities.

See Pokahoe.
REF: *HU:85,201: Il:234; M45; MO:31; SC:310.*

Pennybridge [bridge]

This was the name of the bridge after which the district of Pennybridge was named. See the map of 1891 [M40] in Canning [CA]. The bridge is indicated on this map where Broadway crosses Sheldon Brook. The story goes that, at one time, there was a one penny toll bridge at this site. See Pennybridge [a district].
REF: *M40.*

Pennybridge [district]

Generally speaking, Pennybridge is that portion of the Village of Tarrytown lying south of Tarrytown Road and north of Glenwolde Park. It is said to have been named for a one penny toll bridge which at one time spanned Sheldon Brook at Broadway. The Pennybridge district evolved from the Revolutionary farm of Gerrit Van Weert.

Canning [CA] offers some interesting information about early days in Pennybridge.
REF: CA:97,118,238; LE:110; M33[COL:129]; M42; TAR:40.

Pennybridge Brook, the
See Sheldon Brook and Mill Brook.
REF: WO:31[cap].

Petticoat Lane
The first written occurrence of this place name may have been in Irving's 1809 historical satire, *A History of New York*: "...the mighty men of battle of Tappan Bay—and the brave boys of Tarry-Town, Petticoat-Lane, and Sleepy-Hollow...." [IR:651]   Irving mentions the name again in "Wolfert's Roost": "...Jacob Van Tassel, with the holy brotherhood of Tarrytown, Petticoat Lane and Sleepy Hollow...." [IR:304]

John Odell was among the most renowned of the "Westchester Guides" during the Revolution.   The guides were an elite group of mounted soldiers whose excellent knowledge of Westchester terrain enabled them to lead American forces into enemy territory.   The story goes that Odell had scattered a party of Cowboys (Loyalist troops) from a house which still stands along Route 119 near Glenville, and it was necessary for him to remain there for the night.   The next day, upon the arrival of his commanding officer, Colonel Sheldon, Odell could not locate his breeches. The lady of the house supplied him with a petticoat, a circumstance which inspired the name of the road.   In another version of the story, Odell dresses in woman's attire to escape the notice of an enemy party surrounding the house.

Today the house alluded to in the story is still used as an antique store.   It can be found on the old section of Route 119 just west and across from the Marriott Hotel.   A map of 1891 (in HUT) shows Tarrytown Road labeled as Petticoat Lane.   In Raymond [RA], the house is referred to as the "old McCormick house, still standing on the White Plains Road, about one mile this side of Halls Corners [Elmsford]...."

Note that Petticoat Lane (Route 119) has occasionally been mistaken for the "Lower Crossroads."   To be precise, Route 100C was most commonly known as the Lower Crossroads.
VAR: Petticoat-Lane.

REF: BAC:217; CA:201; IR:304,651; M35; M42; M57; RA:83; WO:23-24.

Phelps Place

It is not clear which member of the Phelps family purchased this estate and built the "James House." According to Canning [CA], this estate on the north side of Pokahoe was purchased by Anson G. Phelps (1781-1853) from the Beekman family. It has been also described [JAM] as a sixty-six-acre estate purchased by William Phelps (d.1858) and his wife, Jane Gibson Phelps, in 1848. Miller [MI] and Hutchinson [HU] write that Mrs. Jane G. Phelps was the widow of Anson G. Phelps. A pamphlet on the subject of the James House [JAM] notes that Anson G. Phelps II built the house in 1851. According to the *Dictionary of American Biography* [DI], Anson G. Phelps, the founder of Phelps-Dodge, was married to Olivia Eggleston and had seven daughters and one son.

Whatever is the case, in the late nineteenth century the estate was owned by Jane Phelps, who lived there with her sister Miss Helen Louise Gibson. Jane Phelps remained there until her death in 1909. Miss Gibson continued to reside there until her death in 1918. Then the estate passed into the hands of Arthur Curtiss James, a nephew of Anson G. Phelps II [according to JAM]. Subsequently, a large part of the estate became the grounds of Phelps Memorial Hospital.

The estate's mansion, the James House, offers fine views of the Hudson River and is frequently used for conferences and receptions. By the 1890s, Jane Phelps's landholdings in this area were extensive. In addition to this parcel, she held another one hundred acres directly across Broadway and 140 acres in Pocantico Hills.

Anson G. Phelps, William E. Dodge, and Daniel James were partners in Phelps, Dodge & Company. William E. Dodge was married to Melissa Phelps Dodge.

VAR: Phelps Estate.
REF: CA:236; DI:Vol.7,p525-526; HU:83; M40; M41; JAM; M45; MI:21; ZU:105.

Pierson Park

This is a village park on the Tarrytown waterfront. The park has a picnic area, tennis, basketball, and platform tennis courts, as well as a playground. It offers beautiful views of the Tappan Zee and the neighboring marina.

The park is located to the west of where André Brook connects with the Hudson at Tarrytown Harbor.

REF: DAI:36; GE:48; M58; NE [Aug. 21 1994].

Philipsburgh Manor

This was the vast tract of land purchased by Frederick Philipse I (d. 1702) from local Native American tribes and others. His holdings were chartered as a manor (a political unit) by the British Crown in 1693. Philipsburgh is referred to in the Royal Charter as Philipsborough, and that name along with many other variations of it are generally used to describe the collective Westchester holdings of Philipse. Philipse Manor was one of six "freehold manors" created by the Crown in the county of Westchester. Philipse's manor was confirmed by the English Crown during the administration of British Governor Fletcher. Together, Philipse's land grants and purchases comprised much of western Westchester County, roughly 90,000 acres (COR gives 165,000 acres).

The land encompassed by the modern villages of Sleepy Hollow and Tarrytown was, of course, part of this "manor," as was all of present day Mount Pleasant and Greenburgh. The site of Philipse's original manor house, mill, and church on the Pocantico was an important early nucleus for the activities of the manor. [See BOL for the complete "Royal Charter" of Philipsburgh.]

Philipse also owned some salt meadows (the "Tappan Meadows") on the west shore of the Tappan Zee, which were said by some to be considered part of Philipsburgh. He held real estate in Manhattan, in other parts of Westchester, and in New Jersey.

Philipse was baptized in 1626 at Bolswaert, Friesland, in the Netherlands. He may have arrived in New Amsterdam on the same ship as Governor Peter Stuyvesant in 1647. After working for a time as a carpenter and appraiser for Stuyvesant, he entered the shipping trade. Upon the English seizure of the New Netherlands in 1664, Philipse made a smooth transition by cultivating good relations with the new government. By 1674 he was said to be the wealthiest man in New York. From 1675 to 1698 Philipse served on the influential Governor's Council.

He was married twice, first in 1659 to Margaret Hardenbrook

De Vries, the widow of Peter Rudolphus De Vries, a New Amsterdam merchant and trader. Margaret was an active and prosperous businesswoman, operating her own ships between New Amsterdam and Europe. She died sometime before 1692. Philipse's second wife also brought him a considerable fortune. Catherine van Cortlandt was a widow, too, and the daughter of Oloff Stevensz van Cortlandt, the founder of the powerful van Cortlandt family in New York.

The Philipse interests prospered throughout the late seventeenth century. In Albany he was the leading trader with the Iroquois, and he had a highly profitable trade in slaves between Madagascar, the West Indies, and New York. He was closely connected to a long line of British governors of New York who were especially generous to him, particularly in the matter of Hudson River land grants.

Philipse was a shrewd businessman who was both fortunate and farseeing in his dealings with the political leaders of New York. But his successful run was at least briefly interrupted in 1698, when he and his son Adolphus lost the protection of the New York governor, the Earl of Bellomont. Frederick and Adolphus Philipse were accused of smuggling:

> ...[his] great concerns in illegal trade are not only the subject of common fame but are fully and particularly proved....

So wrote the British Board of Trade to the British Lord Justices regarding Philipse. This led to an official order removing Frederick Philipse from the New York Council "and from all other places of publick trust within that government...." If Philipse was indeed a smuggler, he was no doubt a very successful one. He had all the resources necessary: ships, capital, and trading partners. In fairness, smuggling in the colonial period was so common as to be nearly an all-American activity.

The Earl of Bellomont also complained to the Lords of Trade that earlier governors of New York had extended to Philipsburgh the right, after twenty years, to elect representatives to the colonial assembly. He pointed out that Philipse had only about twenty families of poor tenants on his land. Bellomont mentions, too, that Adolphus Philipse had no tenants at all on his Highland Patent. (The Great Highland Patent was a land grant twenty miles by twelve miles, including all of Putnam County. It was granted to Adolphus Philipse in 1697 for a yearly rent of 20 shillings.)

It appears that in settling farmers upon his lands, Frederick Philipse I granted some leases forever, some for 999 years, some for 99 years, and some for "three lives." The tenants could sell their leases, but Philipse was to receive a portion of the proceeds. Occasionally his descendant, Frederick III, would buy tenants out, sometimes using their debts and imprisonment to soften the tenant's bargaining position. It is not clear whether the lord of the manor had the option to raise rents at will, or whether there was some provision in the original leases which governed increases. Apparently, Philipse did not have the option to throw his tenants out. See EA for more.

Frederick Philipse III (d. 1785) was the son of Frederick Philipse II (d. 1751) and the great-grandson of Frederick Philipse I (d. 1702). The second Frederick was the son of Phillip, Frederick I's first son.

During the Revolution, Philipse cast his lot with the British. As a result, his lands were confiscated by the State of New York and sold. Following the Revolution, a British Royal Commission was set up to investigate the losses of Loyalists during the Revolution. The records concerning the losses of Frederick Philipse III supply detailed information about Philipsburgh's value and the economic relations between tenant and landlord. Here we see a financial snapshot of Philipsburgh's tenants and rents.

Philipse's claim for losses in rents, bonds, notes, interest, and property between 1776 and 1784 was more than 40,000 pounds sterling. In addition, friends of Philipse fixed the value of his "life interest" in Philipsburgh Manor at between 100,000 and 150,000 pounds sterling, a fraction of the manor's total worth. The witnesses add that had Philipse been entitled to ownership in "fee simple," Philipsburgh might have been worth between 260,000 and 290,000 pounds sterling. This demonstrates that Philipse had been one of the richest men in the colonies.

Before the Revolution, Philipsburgh had 280 tenants. Rents were fixed between approximately one pound and two hundred pounds. In addition, fifty tenants owed money (principal and interest) to Frederick Philipse III. As a landlord, Philipse was characterized as "mildly paternalistic." His title was such that he could not sell his land, but must pass it along to future heirs.

The manor had a local government of trustees, town supervisors, fence-viewers, superintendents of highways, and overseers of the poor. Westchester County required that one own property worth at least sixty pounds in order to serve on a jury. This meant that most tenants of Philipsburgh were excluded. A freehold worth forty pounds was required for a man to vote.

Countryman [COU] suggests that of 283 male tenants, seventy-six were decidedly Loyalist and forty-three were decidedly revolutionaries; the majority remained neutral. Most of those with low rents became revolutionaries, and most of those with high rents became Loyalists.

Philipse had restrictions on his ability to dispossess his tenants, but he may have been at liberty to increase their rents. It seems that he voluntarily put a cap on rents during his lifetime, but that tenants could expect significant increases upon the transfer of the manor to his heirs. Many of the tenants who favored independence owed Philipse money. They were later to buy their tenant farms from the New York State Commissioners of Forfeiture. Philipsburgh Manor was reportedly sold to 287 individuals after the Revolution.

After spending the latter part of the Revolution in the British stronghold of New York, Philipse moved with his family to England. He died in Chester, England, in 1785.

For a detailed account of the rise of Philipsburgh, see Shonnard [SH]. See Dankers and Sluyter [DAN] for more on the story of the Philipse family.

See Philipse Manor, Upper Philipsburgh, and the Upper Mills.

VAR: *Philips Borough, Philipsborough, Philipsburg, Philipseburg, Philipsburgh, Philipsburgh Manor, The Manor of Philipsburgh, The Manor of Philips Burgh, Manor of Phillipsburgh [sic - IN, M17], old Philipse Manor, Philipseborough, Philipsborough, Philipseborough, Philipseburgh, Philipseburgh Manor, Philipse manor, Philipse Manor; Philipsburg Manor, Philips-Bourgh, Mannour of Philipsborough, Manor of Philipsborough.*

REF: *BAC:219; BOL:vol.II,589-598; CA:24-6; CON:27,28,37; COR:np; COU:np; DA2 [Mar. 12 1937]; DAI:31; DAN:258,353,362-365; DE:3-4; DU:4; EA:99-137; FI:vii,1,4,155-177; GE:10; GR:48; ; HA:72; HAD1:37; HIN:272; HIS:n.p.; HISTOR:np; HO:140,137; HU:9,19,21,22; HUT:26-27,29IN:40; JE:346; LE:111; M4; M16; M17; M44; MI:3; OC:[vol.4]390,411,535 [vol.8]735; OE:18; OW:22; PHIL:np; PHIL1:8-21; RA:21,47,62,91,108; SH:156-163,255-263,527 ;TAR:1; TWO:114,126,132; WES:Vol.12,No.4, 85-86,95.*

Philipsburg Manor—Upper Mills

This name is applied to the modern restoration of the Upper Mills. A restoration was first opened to the public in 1943 under the name of the Philipse Castle Restoration. It was paid for largely by John D. Rockefeller, Jr., other members of the Rockefeller family, and Mrs. Worcester Warner and her daughter Helen. In a 1943 newspaper article, the Rockefeller donations were estimated to exceed $200,000.

Ownership of the land was subsequently conveyed to Sleepy Hollow Restorations (Historic Hudson Valley).

A new and more extensive restoration opened in 1969, after an archaeological excavation of the site. The historic attraction is currently restored to the period of Adolph Philipse's early eighteenth century tenure. The restoration constitutes about twenty acres; the Upper Mills establishment of mid-eighteenth-century Philipsburgh encompassed about 720 acres.

See Castle Philipse, Philipse Castle, Upper Mills.

VAR: Philipsburg Manor, Upper Mills, Philipsburg Manor Upper Mills, Philipsburgh Manor, Upper Mills of Philipsburg Manor, Philipse Castle Restoration.

REF: CAL2; DA2 [Jan. 25 1943]; GE:25-26; GET:22; GM:7 & pic; HHV1; M20:26; MO:33; NE [Aug. 21 1994]; OW:3,14; P4; PHIL:np; TAR:2,38; YE:np; ZU:92-95.

Philipse Castle

See Castle Philipse.

VAR: Philipse's castle, Philipse's Castle, Philipse Castle Restoration; Philipse Castle Manor House.

REF: DA2 [Mar. 12 1937]; FI:np[pic]; GR:51; HO:140; JE:381; M20:26; M42; M44; MO:4,26; PE1: vol.24/3 328; PHI:np; TA:11; TAP:np; TN [Oct. 31 1996].

Philipse Church

See Old Dutch Church of Sleepy Hollow, Sleepy Hollow Church.

REF: PHI:np.

Philipse Manor

This is an early twentieth-century residential development. It was created on lands which had formerly belonged to the Kingsland estate. The neighborhood is bordered by Broadway on the east, the

Philipsburg Manor—Upper Mills
Mill, manor house (Castle Philipse) and Dutch barn. Photo by Henry Steiner.

Hudson River on the west, Sleepy Hollow Manor to the north, and the Pocantico River to the south. Philipse Manor is named for the manor of Philipsburgh [see above], of which it was once a part.

At the turn of the twentieth century, the Mobile Corporation of America bought this parcel of land and Kingsland Point from the Kingsland family. The point was used as a site for Mobile's steam automobile factory, and the balance of the property was earmarked as a residential development under the name of Philipse Manor-on-the-Hudson. The residential plan faltered, but an associate of the Mobile Corporation, Dr. William Bell, organized the Philipse Manor Company and proceeded with development about 1910.

In January 1914, the property was "swapped" for a New York City skyscraper located at the northeast corner of Fifth Avenue and 31st Street. The new owner of Philipse Manor was the 303 Fifth Avenue Corporation. The company's president, Campbell Carrington, promptly threw a party for the governors of the Philipse Manor Club and Philipse Manor residents. But only eight months after this purchase, Philipse Manor was sold again, this time to a syndicate of Westchester County businessmen. The Robert E. Farley Organization took over sales and management of the development. A neighborhood association, the Philipse Manor Improvement Association was incorporated in 1926.

See also Beekman's Forest, the forty acre lot.

VAR: *the Manor.*
REF: CA:174; CON:7; DA [Mar. 28 1914], [Sept. 14 & 28 1914], [Feb. 14 1914], [Apr. 3 1914], [Jan. 7 1914]; DA2 [July 3 1937], [Sept. 12 1942]; GET:13; HA:102; HU:85,183-185,189; M19; M29; M38; M45; MO:1; PH:np; RO:5; TA:map; TAR:38,40.

Philipse Manor Beach Club

This is a private recreational facility at the Philipse Manor riverfront. The land is owned by the Philipse Manor Improvement Association and leased by the club. This parcel was, for a time, handed over to the Village of North Tarrytown (Sleepy Hollow) and subsequently handed back to the PMIA. The club was one of the amenities originally offered by the developer of Philipse Manor. It includes a small beach and marina.

A photograph of 1917 shows the original clubhouse on the tip of the tiny peninsula; it was subsequently destroyed by fire. There are

several early photographs of the beach club in the picture collection of the Westchester Historical Society.
>   See Philipse Manor.
VAR: *Philipse Manor Boat Club; Philipse Manor Club.*
REF: *CA:174; M38; PH:np; TAR:45.*

Philipse Manor-House
>   See Castle Philipse and Philipse Castle.
VAR: *Philipse Manor House, the Manor House of Upper Philipsburgh, Manor House.*
REF: *M29; PH:np; SC:194; TWO:121,122,131,132.*

Philipse Manor Station
This is a twentieth century train station located in Philipse Manor near the Hudson River. The station was built in 1910, according to a brochure of the Hudson Valley Writer's Center. It was constructed by the developers of Philipse Manor and presented to the railroad as an incentive to schedule passenger train stops at the development. The area of the station was formerly a stone quarry. See TN for a 1910 photograph of River Road near the site of the station.

The station house is listed in the National Register of Historic Places. In recent years, the station house sat vacant and derelict. After extensive renovations in 1996, the station house became the headquarters of the Hudson Valley Writers Center the same year. The center began by sponsoring a series of readings in 1983; it nurtures writers in many genres and offers a forum for their work. Today, this organization sponsors readings, performances, publications, and educational events.

VAR: *Philipse Manor Railroad Station, Philipse Manor station.*
REF: *CH:Summer,1994(No.22); DA2 [Dec. 26 1942]; HU:185[pic],232; I1; M38; M43; MO:10; PH:np; TAR:37; TN [Nov. 22 1996 & pic] [Oct. 31 1996], [Oct. 18 1996], [Oct. 2 1996], [May 10 1996], [Jan. 25 1995 & pic].*

Philipse-his-Castle
According to Hanson, this name for Castle Philipse was used in colonial times.
>   See Castle Philipse.
VAR: *Flypse—his Castle.*
REF: *BA:37; HA:66.*

Pine Tree Lot, the
   See Wolf Hill, Edgemont, Detmer Estate, Sigafus Estate.
REF: *RAY:11.*

Pinkstone
   Pinkstone was the name of the thirty-five-acre John T. Terry (b. 1822) estate; it was located north of Lyndhurst. Terry was an influential lawyer who served on many corporate boards, including that of Western Union. He was doubtlessly an associate of Jay Gould, his neighbor to the south. The Terry mansion which stood at Pinkstone was built in 1859.
REF: *M29; M35; M40; SC:243[& pic].*

Pleasance
   W. S. Wilson had a fourteen-acre estate east of Beech Lane and south of Earlston. (See map of 1891 [M40].) It carried eastward to where the Upper Lake now lies. Lederer [LE] disagrees on the matter of size. He writes that it encompassed twenty acres including a vineyard and orchard. A map of 1868 [M38] shows that Wilson was already residing at the place by that date.
   When the writer was a child living on Walden Road, he played baseball in the small, sloped Wilson Park lot at the foot of Walden Road. Baseball could also be played further east on the athletic field of Marymount secondary school which bordered the lake. In the fall one could pick fruit from one of the neglected apple trees which were, no doubt, planted during Mr. Wilson's tenure. The trees stood along the driveway leading to the field.
   See Wilson Park.
REF: *LE:(addendum); M35; M40; M56.*

Pocantico
   This name is said to be derived from the Algonquian, meaning "river that runs between two hills."
   See Pocantico River, Mill River, Sleepy Hollow Brook.
REF: *BAC:216; BO:316; BOL:vol.I,505; GR:51; HI:20; HIN:272; IRVIN:107; LE:113.*

Pocantico Bay
   This was Lossing's term for *Slapershaven* when he wrote in the

1860s. The term describes a place which was later to become the General Motors site.
See *Slapershaven*.
REF: LO:327.

Pocantico Brook
This was a nineteenth century name for the Pocantico River. John Romer used the term in 1848. See map of 1891 [M40].
See Pocantico River.
REF: M8; M40; MA:851; RA:165; SC:306.

Pocantico Creek
In 1684 Governor Dongan used this place name in the land grant confirming the holdings of Frederick Philipse I. A map of 1864 [M62] also includes the name.
See Pocantico River.
VAR: *Pocantico Creeke, Pocantige Creek, Pocantico Kill or Creek.*
REF: CRA:166; GR:48; HU:11; M62; TA:map.

Pocantico Grove
Pocantico Grove constituted much of the northern portion of what is today Sleepy Hollow Cemetery. In the 1870s and 1880s, this hillside was the summer estate of G. F. Saachi. Prior to that, it served as a Methodist meeting ground from 1841. One source mentions that vandalizing Connecticut cavalry troopers camped here during the Civil War. The name obviously derives from the Pocantico River.
REF: HU:72; SC:309; TN [Oct. 31 1996].

Pocantico Hills*
This Mount Pleasant hamlet stands west of the summit of Buttermilk Hill. It began to develop as a residential area in the 1860s and 1870s, when it was known as Tarrytown Heights. A New York and Northern train schedule in Hutchinson [HUT] shows that, by 1893, the station stop in this district was known as "Pocantico Hills" (although Tarrytown Heights appears in parentheses).

Owens [OW] discusses how the advent of the Putnam Valley and Great Northern Railroad in 1880-1881 triggered the growth of Pocantico Hills as a hamlet. A train station once stood near the site of the Union Church. The settlement began as a summer colony with growing retail businesses. During the 1880s a large-scale plan to build a residential community at Pocantico Hills failed, disappointing several local investors.

John D. Rockefeller purchased a considerable amount of acreage in Pocantico Hills during the 1890s. He embarked on an ambitious program of improvements to his estate, but also customized public features to his tastes. He was responsible for having the railroad re-routed away from Pocantico Hills and had curves put into neighboring roads; houses were moved to the center of the community from outlying areas. The *Tarrytown Daily News* of November 1930 reported that John D. Rockefeller, Jr., was embarking on plans to create a "model village" in Pocantico Hills. This was to include churches, schools, a library, and a swimming pool. Members of the Rockefeller family have exerted considerable control over the growth and development of the community and made significant contributions to its religious and cultural institutions.

Conklin [CON] writes that the Pocantico Hills area was rich in flint used by early Native Americans for their stone tools and weapons.

See Tarrytown Heights (Pocantico Hills).

REF: BI:np; CON:7,24; DA2: [Nov. 12 1930], [May 24 1937]; DE:1; GR:51; HUT:85; M19; M29; M45; OW:20,23; SC:305; WES:Vol.32, No. 4.

Pocantico Lake*

The lake was obviously named after the Pocantico River. Hutchinson [HU] relates that this was the fresh water source for the Village of North Tarrytown (Sleepy Hollow) through 1926. Pocantico Lake is near Briarcliff, just north of Route 117.

See Pocantico River.

REF: HU:100,211; M20:27: M19; WES:Vol.32, No. 4.

Pocantico Pond

The granddaughter of Seth Bird, Mrs. George Mellows, recalled that in the late nineteenth century, during her childhood days, the Mill Pond was known as Pocantico Pond. Her father owned Lovatt's silk mill on the south side of the mill dam. It stood opposite the Philipse grist mill, then owned by Ambrose Kingsland.

REF: HU:99-100; MO:23.

Pocantico Purchase, the

On April 1, 1680, New York Governor Dongan granted lands to Frederick Philipse extending 400 rods along each side of the Pocantico River. The grant confirmed the purchase which Philipse had made from the local Indians earlier that year. The grant can be found in Bolton [BOL:vol. I, page 506].

There was a subsequent Philipse purchase from Native American tribes, dated December 10, 1681. These lands extended from the Pocantico to Sunnyside Brook. (Biseghtick Creek). See Bolton [BOL:vol. I, page 268]. This later purchase was named for the Pocantico River. The land became a part of the Manor of Philipsburgh.

VAR: *the Pocantico tract.*
REF: *BA:8; BOL:vol.I   268-269,506-507;   HO:140;   SH:156; WES:Vol.12,No.4,p.85.*

Pocantico River

The name Pocantico is from the Algonquian, meaning "a swift run between high hills." This river begins at Pocantico Lake and empties into the Hudson River at the north end of Kingsland Point Park. The lower portion of the river valley is Sleepy Hollow, famous in legend.

Prior to the twentieth century the river emptied into the Hudson south of Kingsland Point. It formed a bay called *Slapershaven* by the colonial Dutch. Many corruptions of the Dutch name can be found.

Like other rivers, the Pocantico served as an ancient boundary for American Indians, the Dutch, and the English. The river passes through Sleepy Hollow Cemetery and powers the mill at Philipsburg Manor Restoration.

The Pocantico River Valley abounds with a variety of wildlife, both aquatic and terrestrial. A long stretch of the upper river valley runs through the vast Rockefeller Preserve, where hawks and deer are easily observed. In 1996, the Village of Sleepy Hollow began a trout stocking program upstream of Route 9. The stream bed was improved as a trout habitat at several points within Sleepy Hollow Cemetery, and fishing has been improved to the conditions of the early nineteenth century. The village has begun to host regular "fishing derbies" for children.

See Pocantico, *Slapershaven,* Slaeperig Haven, Sleepy Hollow,

Pocantico Creek, Pocantico Brook.
VAR: Pocantico, Pekantico, Pocanteco, Pekantico, Pueghanduck; Po-cante-co.
REF: BOL:vol.I,268; COLL:3,4; CON:7; DE:1; HA:25; HAR [Apr. 1876, p. 643]; HO:138; HU:2; IR:298-299,311; LO:319; M2; M20:26; M21; M29; M35; M42; M45; M65; MI:7; OW:6; RO:np; TA:9; TAR:1; SL:np; TN [June 21 1996 & pic], [Oct. 18 1996]; WO:10; YE:np.

Pocantico Suburb, the

This name served as an alternate name for Beekmantown in the mid-nineteenth century. The Pocantico Suburb was, of course, named for the nearby Pocantico River.

Beekmantown, which comprised a small portion of today's Village of Sleepy Hollow, was considered a "suburb" of Tarrytown in the mid-1800s. The historic hamlet of Sleepy Hollow lay to the north of Beekmantown.

See Beekmantown.
REF: BO:327; BOL:vol.I,531; HU:58; SH:591.

Pocantico Vale, the

This name was applied to that portion of the Pocantico River valley near the Old Dutch Church.
REF: IN:55.

Pockerhoe

Bolton writes that this place name has the same origins as the name Pocantico. It is said to derive from the Algonquian term, *Pockohantes*, meaning a "run between two hills."

See Hokohongus and Pokahoe.
REF: BO:316; BOL:vol.I,505; LE:114.

Point Cove

The sandy, crescent-shaped beach at Kingsland Point had this name. According to Hutchinson [HU], there is a tradition that Henry Clay enjoyed walking here while visiting fellow politician Ambrose C. Kingsland.
REF: HU:85,183.

Point Landing

In the nineteenth century there was a landing on Tarrytown Point at the foot of Main Street. It was established in 1801 and managed by Jacob Couenhoven, who owned a storehouse nearby. As early as 1867, maps show the landing extending west of the railroad tracks, a terminus for the Nyack ferry.

See Steamboat Landing, Tarrytown Point.

VAR: Point Dock, Point Dock Landing, Tarrytown Terminal Dock, Tarrytown Terminal Corporation dock.
REF: CA:47,204; DA2 [June 7 1930], [June 18 1942]; M34; M38; M40; RA:86; SC:194.

Pokahoe

This was the estate of newspaperman General James Watson Webb (1802-1884), who purchased the land from the estate of Gerard G. Beekman in 1845 or 1846 and lived here until 1861. Webb joined the army at age seventeen and experienced some interesting youthful adventures in the West. He entered the newspaper business in the 1820s, pursuing an active and controversial career. In the 1860s, he served for eight years as United States minister to Brazil. Washington Irving and Commodore Perry were frequent guests at Pokahoe during Webb's ownership of the estate. It was Webb who named the house and estate Pokahoe; he may have been inspired by the tradition that this was the name of an ancient Indian village located at the site. [See Hokohongus.]

According to a new book, *Images of America Tarrytown and Sleepy Hollow*, Webb sold his estate of 53 acres to Ambrose Kingsland in 1864, and it was then resold the next year to presidential candidate, soldier and explorer, General John C. "The Pathfinder" Frémont. Frémont later sold the estate to Elbert C. Munroe [in 1875?], who used it as a country home. Much of the land ultimately became the twentieth century residential development of Sleepy Hollow Manor. For a time, the house was used as the sales office for Sleepy Hollow Manor. The house, built in 1848, is still standing, although it is missing two of its original stories.

See Fremont Fountain, Fremont Pond, Pockerhoe.

VAR: Pocahoe, Pocaho, Pockerhoe, Pokerhoe.
REF: AND:35; BA:69; CA:234; DI:Vol.X,p574-575; HU:83; JE:369; LO:319; SC:310; TA:33; TN [Nov. 29 1996]; WES:6:42-44; WES

[Fall 1991, p. 76]; WI:154-155.

Post Office Hill

This was the hill extending from Depot Plaza to where Main Street and White Street divide. The post office was here by 1867 [see M38]. After 1886, the post office was located near the division of those roads in the building now occupied by Goldberg Hardware. Over time, the post office has been located in several places along Main Street.

REF: CA:67; LE:15; M38; TARR:np.

Prospect Hill

Prospect Hill has also been known as Cedar Hill and Jones Hill. Long View, the thirty-eight-acre estate of Henry L. Douglas, stood on Prospect Hill east of the Old Croton Aqueduct and south of the G. S. Rice estate in 1891. Douglas first came to this area in 1868. He had been successfully engaged in business in San Francisco from 1851 to 1857. The Douglas Estate also bordered that of S. T. Thayer, stockbroker and poet. Douglas Park is dedicated to the brother of H. L. Douglas, John W. Douglas (d.1883). The *Tarrytown Argus* [AR] of September 29, 1883, noted the death of John W. Douglas. When H. L Douglas died on May 6, 1887, he left two sons, Archy and Percy, and a daughter, Catherine Waldo Douglas.

The name Prospect Hill was apparently in use before the H. L. Douglas tenure; see the map of 1864 [M62]. Scharf suggests that the hill was used for reconnaissance by Washington and that it was a lookout for local Indians prior to European settlement.

See Cedar Hill, Jones Hill and Douglas Park.

REF: AR [Sept. 29 1883], [May 7 1887]; LE:116; M17; M40; M57; M62; MI:17; MO:27,28; SC:306-307.

Pugsley's Point

An eighteenth century map identifies Kingsland Point by this name. William Pugsley leased the Upper Mills from Frederick Philipse III in 1760. He continued to lease this property, with its large forest, through the time of the War of Independence.

At the time of the Revolution, William Pugsley appears to have paid the highest rent in Philipsburgh, 200 pounds annually. Pugsley occupied one of the largest farms, which included the Upper Mills

establishment. He also was indebted to Frederick Philipse III for more than 49 pounds in principal and interest. Philipse would never collect the debt, due to the Revolution and New York State's confiscation of Philipsburgh. Following the war, in 1785, Gerard Beekman purchased a large portion of Philipsburgh north of André's Brook. Pugsley's Point then became known as Beekman's Point.
See Beekman's Point, Kingsland Point.
REF: DE:4; EA:120: HU:85; M11; PE1: vol.24/3 328; PHI:np.; RAY:16; VAND:[map].

Quarry Castle
This is another name for Centennial Tower. It was so named because it was situated above a quarry at Kelbourne Avenue and the Hudson riverside.
See Centennial Tower.
REF: HU:117.

Quattrociocchi Field
In the early 1990s, a new little league baseball field built at the north end of De Vries Field was named for Joseph Quattrociocchi.
According to an obituary in the Rome *Daily Sentinel,* September 20, 1983, Joseph P. "Joe Quattro" Quattrociocchi (1918-1983) was born at Rome, New York, and educated at North Tarrytown High School, Ithaca College, and Columbia University. He served as an officer in World War II and in the Korean War. From 1948 to 1975, he served as the superintendent of the North Tarrytown (Sleepy Hollow) recreation department.
VAR: Quattro Field, Quatro Field.
REF: ST; STO.

Railroad Station Plaza
See Depot Plaza.
REF: TAR:37.

Raven Rock*
A ghostly woman in white is said to haunt a large rock in Pocantico Hills. According to Lederer [LE], the rock is named for the ravens which were reported to gather there. The rock is in a dark and foreboding glen on the east side of Buttermilk Hill, southeast of

Ferguson Lake.

The story goes that during a snowstorm a woman who had lost her way settled between the rock and the hillside for shelter, and there died of exposure. Whenever it is stormy, her ghost wails and shrieks to warn people away from that dreadful spot. This legend is briefly alluded to in "The Legend of Sleepy Hollow." It is one of the many hair-raising stories served up to Ichabod Crane before the hapless schoolmaster's encounter with the Headless Horseman.

Alternately, there is a story of an Indian maid who was killed when her jealous lover pushed her off the rock. Passers-by can still hear her cries echoing through the rocks on stormy nights. There is still another legend of a woman who, in the days of the Revolution, went there to escape the unwelcome amorous advances of a Tory raider.

In the *Westchester Historian* [WES], we are told that Raven Rock was also known as crow's rock: "[It] is an unusual arrangement of rocks with perpendicular walls, deep crevices and an old cave that has almost or completely disappeared." Bolton [BOL] writes that ravens are traditionally birds of ill omen. A raven's screech forecasts doom. It seems that the bird became quite rare in Westchester in the late nineteenth century.

REF: BA:111-113; BOL:vol.I p.551; BOL:vol.II p.123; CON:24; IR:41; LE:118; OW:23; WES:Vol.32, No. 4; WIL:[pic].

Reed's Tavern

Isaac Reed purchased a farm of 124 acres from the New York State Commissioners of Forfeiture immediately after the Revolution. It seems that he occupied this land as a tenant before he purchased it and subsequently operated a tavern there. Reed's Tavern was later known as the Landrine House. William Landrine bought the house from the Reed family in 1824. A picture of it can be seen in Scharf [SC].

The house stood on the north side of County House Road at Tarrytown Lakes on land which was later to be purchased by John D. Rockefeller, Sr. It was located about a half mile from East View Station and a half mile from Tarrytown Heights Station. Scharf indicates that the house was plainly visible from Tarrytown Heights Station at the south end of the Tarrytown Lakes. Reed's Tavern was torn down at the turn of the twentieth century.

It was to this home that Major André was taken immediately

after he was captured. André was said to have seated himself on the front stoop to rest after his capture; the original stoop was preserved for many years by the owners of the house. The property belonged for a time to Ambrose Kingsland before it was acquired by John D. Rockefeller, Sr.

REF: AB:88; ABB:[pic. opp. p.32]; BA:127,136; HIS:33; HUF:[map]; M1; M35; M42; RA:177; SC:205-206; WES:Vol.32, No. 4.

Refugees' Path, the

During the American Revolutionary War, Loyalist soldiers headquartered in lower Westchester were called "the Refugees." Bodies of these troops, like Delancey's Rangers, would strike up-county from their base in lower Westchester (today part of the Bronx). These forces would operate alone or in concert with British and Hessian contingents. The element of surprise was preserved by taking back roads and byways.

John Yerks, one of the larger party of seven who delivered Major John André to American headquarters in 1780, referred to this route in 1845. During his interview with historian John M. MacDonald, Yerks reported that while the three captors intercepted André on the Post Road, Yerks and three others were guarding "the Refugees' path," about three hundred yards to the east.

See Captors' Monument and Neutral Ground.

REF: MC:281; RA:170; YE:np.

Requa-Martling Dock

The dock was named for the Martling and Requa families who operated the waterfront facility and lived in houses nearby. This small hub of local commercial activity was located at the foot of White Street (formerly known as Dock Street) on Tarrytown Bay. It was near this place that the "Action at Tarrytown" occurred on July 15, 1781.

See Martling's Landing, Requa's Brook.

VAR: *Requa's Dock, Old Requa Dock.*
REF: CA:40. M17; M22; M38; M57.

Requa's Brook

A mid-nineteenth century map [M53] shows this brook running through the land now occupied by Lyndhurst. The brook is named for the Requa family. Their homestead was recently excavated by archaeologists during a project coordinated by the Historical Society of the Tarrytowns.

Glode Requa (d. 1806) settled in Tarrytown in the 1720s, as a tenant of Philipse Manor. Born Claude Equier and descended from a French Huguenot who settled in New Rochelle, his name was corrupted by local Dutch and English. Requa commanded a militia company in the Revolution. Later, he acquired his farm from the New York State Commissioners of Forfeiture. One of Glode Requa's sons operated Requa's Dock.

Scharf [SC] referred to the brook as "Jay Gould's spring" in the 1880s.

REF: COLL:27-28; M1; M53; SC:231.

Reverend Sykes Park

This is small park at the foot of Valley Street, at its intersection with Wildey Street. It offers benches, a playground, and a basketball court. Reverend Sykes, a pastor of the Shiloh Baptist Church, played an instrumental role in the establishment of the park.

REF: GE:48; NO:np; NOR:np.

Rice Farm

This appears to have been the ninety-acre parcel of George S. Rice, found on a map of 1893 [M41].

REF: HU:167; M40; M41.

River View

In the late nineteenth century, the estate of G. Ellis was known by this name. It lay where Hitachi headquarters stands today.

REF: M56.

Robertson Square

Dr. John W. Robertson (1859-1928) was a respected local physician who practiced medicine in North Tarrytown (Sleepy Hollow). The square, formerly called Washington Square, was officially renamed in 1959. A monument to Robertson stands on this grassy plot at the juncture of Valley, Washington, and Chestnut Streets. The dedication reads, "In memory of John W. Robertson, M. D. 1859-1928. His unselfish efforts generosity and human understanding will ever inspire us and guide us." There are three other stone memorials on the site.

According to a writer in TN, "Dr. John M. [sic.] Robertson" arrived in the community during the 1890s. He was called to assist in the practice of Dr. J. H. Furman, who was ill at that time.

In 1937, the Italian-American Societies of the Tarrytowns was disappointed in its plans to erect a monument at Columbus Square on Orchard Street. The North Tarrytown (Sleepy Hollow) village board offered this plot to the group as a monument location. It does not appear that the group took advantage of the offer. A monument to Columbus now stands in Patriots Park.

See Washington Square.

REF: CA:294-295; DA [Sept. 10 1937]; HU:116,152; TN [July 19 1996].

Robinwood

This was formerly the estate of William Smith Brown. It extended from Oak Avenue to where the Tarrytown Lakes now lie. In 1891 his mansion stood opposite the top of today's Cobb Lane.

REF: M8; M40; M41.

Rocheaumont

Rocheaumont was an alternate name for Ericstan. The estate was located near Rose Hill Avenue and Neperan Road.

See Ericstan and Castle Ridge.

REF: M56.

Rockefeller Brook

This is the twentieth century name for the brook intersecting Sleepy Hollow Road approximately one quarter of a mile south of the Carl Brook.

See Gebney Brook and Rockefeller estate.

REF: M19; M58; ST.

Rockefeller Cemetery

The Rockefeller family's private cemetery lies just north of Sleepy Hollow Cemetery. It is the final resting place of former New York State Governor and Vice President of the United States, Nelson A. Rockefeller (1908-1979).

REF SL:map.

Rockefeller Estate, the
    This name denotes the estate established in North Tarrytown (Sleepy Hollow) and Pocantico Hills by industrialist, John D. Rockefeller, Sr. (1839-1937). He began to purchase land in the area of the Tarrytowns in 1893. In 1937, the estate passed to Rockefeller's son, John D. Rockefeller, Jr., the noted philanthropist. This extensive estate was home to the children of John D. Rockefeller, Jr., among them Nelson A. Rockefeller, Governor of New York State and afterwards Vice President of the United States. Rockefeller family members were active in many community projects and institutions.
    The estate covered as many as 4,000 acres, much of it extending beyond the villages of Sleepy Hollow and Tarrytown. In recent years, a large portion of the land has been turned over to the State of New York as a preserve.
    See Rockefeller State Park Preserve and Kykuit.
VAR: *Rockefeller estate; the John D. Rockefeller private estate, Estate of John D. Rockefeller; Pocantico Hills Estate.*
REF: *CA:13,218-219; CON:7,37; DE:1,9; DU:8; HU:201; TA:map; TARR:np [& pics.].*

Rockefeller State Park Preserve
    This 800-acre New York State park was donated by the Rockefeller family. It is projected to be expanded to 1,700 acres. This passive use park offers miles of recreational trails for hiking, cross-country skiing, and horseback riding. It includes twenty-four-acre Swan Lake.
    See Rockefeller estate.
REF: *BI:np; DA2:np; GE:27; GET:28; TN [Aug. 2 1996].*

Rockview
    This was formerly the estate of Dublin-born Robert Graves, who was engaged in the wallpapering business. He died in January 1886.
REF: *AR [Jan. 9 1886]; SC:245.*

Rockwood
    A map of 1891 [M40] shows a small portion of William Rockefeller's estate lying within the northern border of the Village of North Tarrytown (Sleepy Hollow). The parcel is located between Gorey Brook and the Pocantico River. In that time Rockwood

extended all the way from the Hudson, east to the Pocantico. William Rockefeller (1841-1922) had purchased the Hudson River portion of the estate from Lloyd Aspinwall, who had given it the name of Rockwood. Rockefeller later renamed the estate Rockwood Hall. According to De Angelis [DE], William Rockefeller's estate comprised 1,000 acres.

The land lying along the Hudson was once a farm (1840-1848) owned by Commodore Alexander Slidell Mackenzie (d.1848). Mackenzie was an accomplished writer and a lead player in the notorious "*Somers* Affair," which was said to have inspired Herman Melville's *Billy Budd*.

The Somers was a state-of-the-art United States military vessel under Mackenzie's command. A mutiny erupted on the ship while it sailed near the coast of Africa. In the course of dealing with this crisis, Mackenzie sentenced three mutineers to be hanged. One of them was the son of John C. Spenser, the Secretary of War. A sensational inquiry was begun after the ship landed in New York.

Prior to Mackenzie's tenure, his estate was part of the post-Revolutionary Beekman holdings. After Mackenzie died, the land was purchased by Mr. and Mrs. Edwin Barlett. The Barletts subsequently sold the land to business partner, William H. Aspinwall, the great railroad builder who died there in January 1878. Aspinwall's son, General Lloyd Aspinwall, then took possession of the property and built a mansion there. The estate was subsequently purchased by William Rockefeller, who doubled the size of the original mansion while maintaining its style. Rockefeller's stone construction at the estate is said to have employed stone cutters from Kilkenny, Ireland. Most of the land now belongs to Laurance Rockefeller.

Commodore Matthew Calbraith Perry (1794-1858) lived on another estate to the north of Rockwood between 1848 and the March of 1852, just prior to his ground-breaking expedition to Japan. Later owners of the Perry estate were George Swords, who was followed by a Mr. Broker, and subsequently General Lloyd Aspinwall who had moved from Rockwood. General Aspinwall was still living at the former Perry estate near the old aqueduct arch in the late 1880s.

VAR: *Rockwood Hall.*
REF: *BI:np; CA:219,222,234; CAL1; DA2 [Apr. 3 1936]; DE:9; JE:381; LO:319; M29; M40; M41; MI:15[cap],20; TA:33; TARR:np; TN [May 3 1996 pic], [Jan. 12 1996 pic]; ZU:107.*

Rocky Beach
Rocky Beach is a little piece of Hudson River frontage at the foot of Van Wart Avenue. Opposite Rocky Beach, on the same small point, is Sandy Beach.
See Sandy Beach.
REF: CA:239; LE:122.

Russell Memorial Fountain
This fountain, which was formerly located at the corner of Benedict Avenue and Broadway, was donated to the community by Mrs. C. Graham Bacon (Clara Russell) in the late nineteenth century. Fountains of this sort disappeared with the advent of the automobile.
See Canning [CA] for more on Russell.
REF: TA:63.

Sandy Beach
See Rocky Beach.
REF: CA:239; LE:126.

Sasachem Brook*
Lederer [LE] describes this as "...the Indian name for the small brook just south of Archville." His source is the Westchester County Historical Society *Quarterly Bulletins* and *The Westchester Historian*.
REF: LE:127.

Saw Mill River*
The Dutch name for this stream was *De Zaag Kill*, or *Zaeg Kil* (Saw Mill River), after the mill established by Adriaen Van der Donck before 1649. The mill was located in Yonkers, at the mouth of the river where Van der Donck had begun a plantation. Later the river powered Frederick Philipse's "Lower Mills" grist mill at Yonkers.
See Nepperhan.
VAR: Sawmill River, Saw-Mill creek.
REF: M20:23; SH:107; TWO:118; VA:iii.; WO:10.

Saw Mill River Valley*
The terrain of the Saw Mill River Valley has for centuries offered a level, if meandering, bed for routes heading north and south. In colonial times Saw Mill River Road (Route 9A) was a primary

north-south route. The river valley was also attractive to the builders of the old Putnam Railroad. In the twentieth century, the Saw Mill River Parkway was constructed along the river's banks.
REF: RA:21; TWO:167.

Shadow Brook
This estate recently belonged to jazz musician, Stan Getz. The name appears on a wrought iron gate to estate at the northwest corner of Route 9 and Sunnyside Lane.
See Willow Brook.
REF: ST.

Sheep Lot
This was a large pasture on Tarrytown Heights (Tarrytown) described in Canning [CA]. It was an athletic field and picnicking ground before the development of the Tarry Crest.
REF: CA:312-313.

Sheldon Brook
This brook was named for Colonel Henry S. Sheldon. (Bolton refers to him as Henry Sheldon, Esq.) In the nineteenth century Sheldon, who had interests in the silk business, owned much of Pennybridge. The estate lay just north of Lyndhurst. Sheldon's home was described as a beautifully appointed "secluded villa" in the Gothic style. The house stood where the Kraft Foods complex stands today.

Sheldon Brook ran through the property, and it was dammed in several places to produce a cascading effect. The stream flowed by the "old Van Weert mill" which in Sheldon's time had been converted into a "Swiss cottage" and boathouse. The brook continued down to the Hudson, ending in a steep fall.

The Van Weert family were the earliest holders of this portion of Philipsburgh. A member of this family sold the land to Sheldon. Their family name has been spelled alternately, Van Wart, Van Weert, Van Weart. Sheldon was no longer living when Bolton's second edition was published in 1881.

A zoological footnote: In his 1980 addendum, Lederer [LE] points out that this brook is "noted as one of the few remaining breeding grounds of Muhlenberg's turtles." We will have to take his word on this.

See Mill Brook and old Van Weert mill.
REF: *CA:69,203,224,238;   BOL:vol.I,293;   HUFE:83,84;   LE:130   & Addendum; M33[COL:129]; M40; M60; SC:297.*

Sigafus Estate
See Edgemont, Pine Tree Lot, Detmer Estate, Wolf Hill.
REF: *WES:Vol.34:16.*

Slapershaven
This is an important local place name. It may be the earliest Dutch precursor of the name Sleepy Hollow. The book in which the name appears, *Beschryvinge Van Nieuw Nederlant*, was published in 1655 and was written by Dutch colonist Adriaen Van der Donck (d.1655). He writes:

Van de Noort-Rivier [heading]
...als de kleyne en groote Esopus, Kats Kil, Slapershaven, Coldedoncks-Kil, ofte Sagh-Kil, De Wappinckes-Kil, &c. Men han ooch...

Van der Donck was to become a leader in New Netherlands. Upon his arrival in the colony, he served as *schout* on the vast Hudson River patroonship of Killian Van Rensselaer. A *schout* was a kind of magistrate or sheriff. For this post he was well qualified by virtue of his training in law at the University of Leyden. Van der Donck was later to serve on a powerful committee opposed to the administration of Peter Stuyvesant. He was also to found a large plantation at Yonkers named Colendonck. In his day, he was possibly the most educated man in New Netherlands and one of only two lawyers in that colony.

Van der Donck fell afoul of New Netherlands Governor Peter Stuyvesant and returned to Holland for redress. There, while his petition before the States-General languished for years, he occupied some of his time in writing a thorough description of the colony, its resources, and its inhabitants. This published work was to become for us an important source of information about the New Netherlands in the 1640s. Unfortunately, Van der Donck's work has never been widely available in the United States, and an English translation, published in 1841, had not been widely available until it was republished by the Syracuse University Press in 1968.

In the nineteenth century translation of Van der Donck's work,

Slapershaven is translated "Sleepy Haven kill." Kill or Kil means river in Dutch. Since the place name applies to a tributary of the Hudson, the translator logically added the word kill or river. The result was that many nineteenth and twentieth century historians appear to have formulated their own deductions of the original term Van der Donck might have used. This has yielded a range of creative, but faulty, alternatives to the original place name. Some of these corruptions may also owe a debt to the usual inaccuracies applied to foreign words passed down through oral traditions.

See Sleepy Hollow, Slaeperingh Haven.
REF: VAN:8.

Slaeperingh Haven

This name and its variations all appear to be corruptions of *Slapershaven*, the term originally used by Van der Donck in the mid-seventeenth century. For more on this, please see the entry above.

A suggestion is made by Bacon that this place, and the *Hafentje* nearby to the north, served as ambuscades from which American "river guards" in their whale boats harassed British shipping during the Revolutionary War.

It has been said that, in the early days of European settlement Slaeperingh Haven was deep enough to admit sloops as high up the Pocantico as the Upper Mills. The slowing of the Pocantico's flow caused by Philipse's mill dam at the Upper Mills was an early factor in the silting up of this bay. However, it is unlikely that the estuarial lower reaches of the Pocantico ever presented a very hospitable harbor for ocean-going ships with their low drafts.

See *Slapershaven* and Sleepy Hollow.
VAR: Die Slaeperingh Haven, Die Slaaperig Hafen, Die Slapering Haven, Slaper Haven, Slaperhaven, Slapering Hafen, Slapershaven, the Slaperingh Haven, Slaperig Hafen, slaperig haven, Die Slaperige Haven; Slappering Haven.
REF: BA:76; BAC:211; HA:101; HU:56,64,170; IN:54; LE:32; LO:319; M17; PE1: vol.24/3 323; TWO:45; VA:10; WESS.

Slaeperigh Hol

This name is said to have been an early Dutch form of the name Sleepy Hollow. Lossing [LO] writes, "...the valley in the vicinity of the old church, through which it flowed, *Slaeperigh Hol*, or Sleepy

Hollow, the scene of Washington Irving's famous legend of that name."
    See *Slapershaven*, Slaeperingh Haven and Sleepy Hollow.
VAR: Slaeprigh Hol.
REF: GR:48; HO:140; LO:320.

Sleepers Haven Kill

    Sleepers Haven is actually the correct translation of the place name *Slapershaven*, the name recorded by seventeenth century colonist Adriaen Van der Donck.
    Lederer's [LE] equation of "Slaper Haven" with "Secondary Harbor" is apparently incorrect.
    See *Slapershaven*.
REF: LE:132; VAN:8.

Sleepy Haven Kill

    This name translated by Jeremiah Johnson in 1841 [see VA], first appears in Van der Donck's *A Description of the New Netherlands* (1655). It is a term applying to the Pocantico River. The "haven" alluded to in the name is *Slapershaven*, also known by its corrupted form, Slaeperingh Haven.
    See *Slapershaven*.
VAR: Sleepy haven Kill, Sleepy Haven kill, Sleepy Haven Kill.
REF: BO:316; BOL:vol.I,505; HI:20; TWO:46; VA:10.

Sleepy Hollow

    Sleepy Hollow is the most famous place name in the villages of Sleepy Hollow and Tarrytown and perhaps in all of Westchester County. Simply put, the name applies to the lower Pocantico River Valley as it passes through the modern Village of Sleepy Hollow. It seems that Washington Irving located the valley of Sleepy Hollow between the Old Dutch Church and the Carl Brook tributary of the Pocantico River.
    Irving made the name famous when he used it in his popular ghost story. The name is familiar to many in the United States and abroad. Irving visited the Tarrytown area as a teenager in the summer of 1798, at which time he and his friend, James K. Paulding, combed the region which Irving was to make famous. (See WES:6:113.) He wrote in later years that the "character of the valley seemed to answer

the name..." and that it was the name itself that led "...me, in my boyish ramblings, into Sleepy Hollow...." Sleepy Hollow has come to symbolize the quintessential, post-Revolutionary American community, frozen in time, still agrarian, and still carrying many vestiges of its colonial past.

The place name Sleepy Hollow is almost certainly a later English derivation of the Dutch name for the mouth of the Pocantico River, *Slapershaven*. This was the name which mid-seventeenth century writer Adriaen Van der Donck applied to the bay where the Pocantico River connected with the Hudson. [For a discussion of this place name, see *Slapershaven*.] Just when the name Sleepy Hollow first emerged is not clear, but Irving used it in his *History of New York* (1809) ten years before it appeared in "The Legend of Sleepy Hollow."

In legend, Sleepy Hollow is a place where supernatural events are apt to occur and where the senses can be deceived. According to Irving's ghost story, the "leading spirit" of the locale is the redoubtable Headless Horseman. Irving credited the story of the Headless Horseman to an old matron of Sleepy Hollow and to a black mill hand whom he had met at Carl's Mill. In the nineteenth century, Sleepy Hollow was sometimes referred to as "The Hollow."

An 1860 New York State census record included in Shonnard [SH] refers to Sleepy Hollow as a hamlet in Mount Pleasant. It was not uncommon in the mid-nineteenth century for Sleepy Hollow to be considered a part of unincorporated Tarrytown. Gleason's Pictorial [P3 & P4] shows the Old Dutch Church of Sleepy Hollow and the Upper Mills as being in Sleepy Hollow, Tarrytown. [See Introduction.] Irving's friend and early collaborator, James K. Paulding, wrote in 1828 that Tarrytown was "...farther distinguished by being within a mile or two from *Sleepy Hollow*...."

See *Slapershaven*, Slaeperingh Haven and Sleepy Hollow Country.

VAR: *The Hollow, Sleepy-Hollow.*
REF: AN2:np;   BA:141,142,145;   BAC:239;   BOL:Map;   BU:32; CA:56,137,145,234,287; CAS:215,499; COLL:3; CON:7,16,25,28-30,33,34,36,37; DU:3,4; GL:np[cap]; GR:48; HA:101; HAD1:37; HAD2:20; HI:20; HIN:282-283; HO:140, 137 & Plate 14&18; HU:46,100,141,156,216;   HUFE:135;   IN:40,53-56;   IR:22,27, 299,310,311,651;   IRVIN:104-113;   IRVING:i,ii,1-14;   LO:320,

Sleepy Hollow Bridge
The latest crossing, built with the sponsorship of William Rockefeller in 1912. Photo by Henry Steiner.

326,328,329,342; M1; M2; M3; M5; M7; M19; M39; M60; M62; MCD:II20, 137; MI:1,22; OE:18;OW:6; P3; P4; PA:115; PE1: vol.24/3 321; PHI:np; RA:13,19; RO:32; SC:306; SH:256,591; TAP:np; TWO:Title page, 50; VAN:8; WA:14,15,38,40,40A; WE:203; WES:Vol.6:72; WES:Vol.32, No. 4; WI:146; WO:31[map]; YE:np.

Sleepy Hollow, Village of

In 1996 the Village of North Tarrytown was renamed the Village of Sleepy Hollow. The historic river valley of the Pocantico, Sleepy Hollow, is a geographic feature within this village.

See Sleepy Hollow and Village of North Tarrytown.

REF: *TN [Dec. 13 1996],[Dec. 20 1996].*

Sleepy Hollow Bridge, the

The Sleepy Hollow Bridge is alternately known as the Headless Horseman Bridge. It spans the Pocantico River at Route 9 near the south gate to Sleepy Hollow Cemetery.

The perennial question asked by hunters of historic sites is, "This is not the bridge from the story, is it?" Indeed, it is not. However, the bridge of Irving's famous story is not simply the preceding bridge, but one of several preceding bridges which stood near the present span.

The current Sleepy Hollow Bridge was constructed with the financial assistance of William Rockefeller in 1912; the bridge is still in use today, having undergone extensive maintenance in 1991. This 1912 bridge was preceded by earlier structures, and for the sake of clarity the following list has been provided:

Bridge A (1912 to present)	This is the present bridge, financed largely by William Rockefeller [See Rockwood]. It is made of stone and is nearly a triangular affair, connecting Broadway (Route 9) and Old Broadway which approaches from the southeast, a former path of the Post Road.
Bridge B (1872 to 1912)	This bridge, according to Hutchinson [HU] and Conklin [CON], was built in 1872 and is pictured in Scharf [SC] and Bacon [BA]. It was made of stone and it crossed the Pocantico between Old Broadway and where the present highway runs

Bridge C (c.1840 to 1872)	past the Old Dutch Church. This bridge was made of wood, and it was constructed shortly before the appearance of the first edition of Bolton's [BO] history of Westchester County. The bridge is pictured in Lossing [LO] and in Howat [HO]. Its construction in the late 1830s may have been occasioned by the building of the old Croton Aqueduct and the rerouting of the Albany Post Road.
Bridge D (? to c.1840)	Bolton refers to an earlier wooden bridge which preceded Bridge C. He writes: "The bridge so famous in goblin story, crossed the hollow, a few yards east of the present structure, the road having been altered within a few years." Note that this statement is repeated in his 1881 edition and that may lead to some confusion. Bridge D had been gone for "a few years" in 1848 when Bolton's first edition appeared. Lossing [LOS], too, observes that Bridge D stood a few yards east or upstream of Bridge C.
Bridge X (c. Revolutionary Period to ?)	This is a crossing shown in maps by Erskine [M12], Colles [M33], and Adams [M32]. A bridge crossed the river directly behind the Old Dutch Church. Abutments are still visible at this site. After crossing to the north, the traveler followed the Post Road down to where the south cemetery gate is located today. The road then swung in front (west side) of the Old Dutch Church and on northward approximately along Broadway's present route.

Whether Bridge D was the crossing we observe in maps of the Revolutionary period is difficult to determine. It seems unlikely that a wooden bridge still standing about 1840 could have endured from the early 1780s. It is also hard to assess from Bolton's description whether Bridge D was located far enough upstream to have been the Revolutionary crossing, Bridge X. There may have been an interim bridge, one which followed the Revolutionary bridge and preceded Bridge D.

In summary, the bridge known as the Sleepy Hollow Bridge has been at least four distinctly different structures. There is also the possibility that after the main crossing had been moved slightly downstream, the original structure (or a rebuilt bridge on the same abutments) remained standing for a time. This would explain the bridge depicted in CA, TARR, and P6, which certainly dates from the mid to late nineteenth century, but bears no resemblance to bridges B or C. The photograph of this bridge included in TARR is said to have been taken before 1895. According to T. Hutchinson in TN, the first stone bridge was built in 1867, and at that time the Post Road was moved to Old Broadway. "But the older one [bridge] lasted into the 1890's...."

The earliest recorded instance of the name, Sleepy Hollow Bridge, appears to be that in the Bolton [BO] edition of 1848.

Those who are curious about the reference to this bridge in "The Legend of Sleepy Hollow" may wish to review it. Irving [IR:42] writes:

> ...not far from the church, was formerly thrown a wooden bridge, the road that led to it, and the bridge itself, were thickly shaded by overhanging trees, which cast a gloom about it, even in the daytime; but occasioned a fearful darkness at night. This was one of the favorite haunts of the headless horseman; and the place where he was most frequently encountered.

If we disregard for the moment that Irving's story is fiction, it may be entertaining to fix a time frame to his story and the bridge described therein. The narrator tells us that his story was played out "some thirty years since." If we take the date of the story's first publication, 1820, as the time in which the narrator is speaking, we may interpret this to mean about 1790. Incidents in the story place it decidedly in post-Revolutionary years. The war has been ended for at least several years. André's Tree is still standing, so the story takes place before 1801 (the year when the tree was leveled by lightning). It appears that the story is set sometime in the 1790s.

See Headless Horseman Bridge for more source information.

VAR: *the old Ichabod bridge.*

REF: *BA:pic. opp. 40; BO:328; BOL:vol.I,531; CA:222. DU:4; SC:306 (Ill.& note); HA:102; HARP:np[pic]; HO:138; HU:103,162[pic]; IN:55; JE:381; LO:321; LOS:191; M12; M32; M33; MI:14; P6; TARR:np [& pic] TN [Oct. 31 1996 & pic], [Sept. 13 1996 & pic], [July 12 1996 & pic].*

Sleepy Hollow Brook

A 1900 magazine article [MI] refers to the Pocantico as Sleepy Hollow Brook. In the nineteenth century Lossing [LO] called it Sleepy Hollow Creek.

VAR: *Sleepy Haven Creek, Sleepy Hollow Creek.*
REF: *LO:320; MI:6[cap],7.*

Sleepy Hollow Cemetery

The cemetery was organized in 1849 under the name of Tarrytown Cemetery. Afterwards, Washington Irving expressed his wish that the cemetery trustees correct their "blunder." In 1865, after Irving's death, the cemetery was renamed. It borders the Pocantico River on the east, the Old Dutch Burying Ground on the south, and Broadway on the west.

Among the notable people interred there is Washington Irving, whose grave is designated a National Historic Landmark. The grave of labor leader Samuel Gompers (1850-1924) lies not far from the cemetery office. William Rockefeller, brother of John D. Rockefeller, Sr. (1839-1937), and fellow partner in the Standard Oil Company, was laid to rest in a massive classical mausoleum near the cemetery's summit. Industrialists Andrew Carnegie (1835-1919) and Walter Chysler (1875-1940) were also interred at the cemetery.

VAR: *Sleepy Hollow Rural Cemetery.*
REF: *CA:309-311; CRA:27; DA2:np; DAI:31; HA:65; HU:30,72,92; JE:384; M7; M20:23; M21; M29; M45; M47; M58; MI:9; MO:9; PE1: vol.24/3 323; PHI:np; RO:np.; SL:np; TA:map.*

Sleepy Hollow Church

See Old Dutch Church of Sleepy Hollow.
REF: *CA:309; GR:51,53; HA:101; HAR [Apr. 1876, p. 643]; IRVIN:112; PE1 vol.24/3 321; PH:np.*

Sleepy Hollow Churchyard

See Old Dutch Burying Ground and Old Dutch Church.

VAR: Sleepy Hollow churchyard.
REF: LOS:187; RA:73.

Sleepy Hollow Country

This is a twentieth century term which has been applied to the region around Sleepy Hollow. It seems to have been invented to imbue Tarrytown, Irvington, and Pocantico Hills with a share in the celebrity of Sleepy Hollow. [See Sleepy Hollow.] Most of the geographical feature known as Sleepy Hollow is in the Village of Sleepy Hollow. Miller [MI] appears to have introduced the Sleepy Hollow Country idea in a 1900 magazine article, and in 1939 Conklin's [CON] use of the term demonstrates how well it had taken hold.

VAR: *The Sleepy Hollow Country, Sleepy Hollow country; Sleepy Hollow Region, the Sleepy Hollow area.*
REF: CAL2; CON:7; DA2 [Apr. 16 1942]; FO:21; HA:65; MI:1,14,22; NOR:np; OW:51[cap.]; PHI:np; TAR:3.

Sleepy Hollow Haven

This is another name from Lossing [LO] for *Slapershaven*.
REF: LO:325.

Sleepy Hollow Landing

A 1995 political flyer announced that North Tarrytown (Sleepy Hollow) Mayor Sean Treacy, Trustee Morris Alter, and United States Senator Daniel P. Moynihan had attended the dedication of North Tarrytown's new marina, Sleepy Hollow Landing. The park has been partially funded with a $600,000 grant from Westchester County. Work on the site had begun by September of 1996. About ten percent (3000 square feet) of the area will be occupied by the Ferry Sloops Organization.

VAR: *Sleepy Hollow Landing Park.*
REF: March 1995 flyer N. Tarrytown Democratic Party; NOR:np; TN [Nov. 15 1996], [Sept. 27 1996], [May 10 1996 pic].

Sleepy Hollow Manor

This is a twentieth century residential development on land formerly owned by General John C. Frémont. Before Frémont's tenure, the estate was owned by General James Watson Webb, a newspaperman. Lederer [LE] dates the development from 1930.

Sleepy Hollow Manor is located north of Philipse Manor and south of Phelps Memorial Hospital.

See Pokahoe.

REF: *CA:233,234; CON:7; GET:13; HU:83,212; LE:132; M19; MO:10; RO:np; TAR:40.*

Sleepy Hollow Mill

Sleepy Hollow Mill was where Washington Irving heard tales of local lore; Irving himself writes that he first heard the story of the Headless Horseman here. From Irving's description of the place in "Wolfert's Roost" and in "Sleepy Hollow," it appears that the mill was a grist mill, not a saw mill as Bacon [BA] suggests. Bacon may have confused the place with Hart's milling establishment.

Some, including Scharf [SC] and Bacon [BA], refer to the mill at the Upper Mills as the "Sleepy Hollow Mill." This is technically incorrect, but understandable, since the district around the Old Dutch Church is a more frequented part of Sleepy Hollow; however, Carl's Mill should be considered the original "Sleepy Hollow Mill."

See Carl's Mill, Hart's Mills.

REF: *BA:141; IRVING:9; IRVIN:110; P1; SC:310 (Ill. opp.).*

Sleepy Hollow Park

This estate, set in the valley of Sleepy Hollow, belonged to John Anderson in the 1870s and 1880s. It lay in what is now Webber Park and Douglas Park, occupying the lower slope of Jones Hill down to the Pocantico. This land was also known as Anderson Park.

See Anderson Park, Webber Park, Douglas Park.

REF: *M37.*

Sleepy Hollow Railroad Station

The Sleepy Hollow Station stood near the northern end of the Tarrytown Loop, on the Putnam Line (New York and Northern Railroad). The station was located at the intersection of County House Road and the railroad line, south of the tracks.

See Tower Hill.

REF: *HU:157; M40; M41.*

Sleepy Hollow School House, the

According to Scharf, the old schoolhouse was located on the

western edge of Glen Loch, the estate of Stephen D. Law, Esq., beside Sleepy Hollow Road. Bacon's map [M42] seems to agree with this.

Mrs. Eliza Ann See, who died in 1883 at the age of ninety-two, reminisced about having attended school at the Sleepy Hollow School House. She recalled that it was located on the east side of Sleepy Hollow Road, just north of the west entrance to the Law estate; it was constructed of logs and built into the bank of a hill. See M40 for the west entrance to Glen Loch.

Hutchinson [HU] relates that the old schoolhouse was rumored to stand between Gorey Brook and Mill Road.

This place name undoubtedly refers to several different schoolhouses of different periods. A map of 1891 [M40] shows a school west of Sleepy Hollow Road and south of what is today designated the Rockefeller Brook. This seems to be the older building of the two pictured on page 142 of Hutchinson [HU]. According to that source, the last Sleepy Hollow School House was built in 1896 and was used until the 1930s.

Part of the interest in this place name is due to the tradition created by "The Legend of Sleepy Hollow" that Ichabod Crane taught school there.

VAR: old schoolhouse of Sleepy Hollow, Sleepy Hollow school-house.
REF: HU:47,78,141,142,216; M42; MI:9; SC:306; TWO:54.

Soldier's Plot

Soldier's Plot is in Sleepy Hollow Cemetery, near the Broadway boundary of the cemetery, between the two main gates. Soldier's Monument, a bronze statue, was dedicated in 1890 to the 240 Union soldiers who hailed from Greenburgh and Mount Pleasant.
REF: HU:108; MO:9.

South Landing

According to Canning [CA], South Landing was another name for Requa's Dock. It should be noted that another dock or landing lay at the foot of Franklin Avenue (today's Van Wart Avenue), and the name could have applied to this landing as well.

See Requa's Dock, Point Landing, Beekman's Landing, North Landing, Steamboat Landing.
REF: CA:63; M38.

South Tarrytown

This was a name for the southern district of Tarrytown, according to a *Tarrytown Daily News* article of 1932.
REF: DA2 [Sept. 28 1932].

Spook Rock*

Though unmarked, this large, flat rock can be found in the Rockefeller Preserve. It is just south of Route 117, east of Witch's Spring Trail. It is associated with the story of a young Indian brave who one night discovered a group of ghostly Indian maidens dancing and reveling on a large rock. He fell in love with one of them and claimed her as his wife. They lived happily for a time and had a child, but one night the lure of her former enchanted life took hold of the woman, and she went off to revel for the night with her former companions. When she returned, she discovered that she had, in fact, been gone for years. Her husband, child, and home were gone.

See the Rockefeller Preserve map [M62] for the rock's location.
REF: BA:97-102; HU:8,9[pic]; M62; OW:6.

Springside

This was the estate of candy manufacturer William Wallace in the 1860s. His land extended along the east side of Broadway, from the First Reformed Church in the north, to the estate of E. J. Blake in the south. Wallace was responsible for the building of the Music Hall theater in Tarrytown, which opened in 1885. The estate appears to have included lands on both sides of the Old Croton Aqueduct. The name, Springside, refers to André Brook.

The estate was sold to Dr. John M. Furman in 1904. Furman had purchased the Irving Institute near Beekman Avenue from David A. Rowe in 1891. After purchasing the Wallace estate, Furman had the school building moved to that site and renamed it the Irving School. In 1955, the Public Schools of the Tarrytowns acquired the land, and Sleepy Hollow High School was built there.
REF: CA:151,177,234; GE:30; HU:88; M18; M38; M40; M41; M56; TN [Dec. 20 1996 & pic].

St. Paul Hill

This is the hill running along Broadway between Lawrence Avenue and New Broadway. It was named for St. Paul's Church,

which was built in 1873 and demolished in 1924. In the years after 1917, the church was a popular recreational center. The congregation of St. Paul's Methodist Episcopal Church was organized in 1839 and first met at Birdsall's Hall on Beekman Avenue.
VAR: St. Paul's Hill.
REF: CA:248; DA2 [May 24 1937], [May 26 1937]; HU:131; RO:27; TN [Aug. 30 1996].

St. Vincent de Paul

This was a charitable institution for children run by a Catholic order. Located on Broadway south of Tappan Landing, it lay across Broadway from Transfiguration Church on the old John D. Archbold estate, Cedar Cliff.

The institution came to Tarrytown some time after 1918.
REF: M19; M45; TA:map; WES:Vol.69,no.1,p.14.

Steamboat Landing

The names Steamboat Landing and Point Landing appear to be synonymous. An 1864 map [M62], an 1867 map [M38], and an 1881 map [M18] clearly depict the landing as the western terminus of Main Street, on Tarrytown Point. M38 shows the Nyack ferry on the same point or landing, but with its own dock, a few yards north of the main dock.

See Point Landing.
REF: CA:63, M18; M38; M62.

Storm Brook

Today this small brook empties into the Upper Lake at its southeast corner. In the days before the making of the Tarrytown Lakes, the stream passed through this valley, finally connecting with the Saw Mill River. It is named for Jacob Storm who, according to Lederer [LE], purchased the land some time about 1879. On August 15, 1887, a bond was passed to turn the valley of the little brook into a reservoir. Lederer adds that a dam was built along the brook in 1888 creating the Tarrytown Lakes.

See Tarrytown Lakes, Wilson Park, Mount Hope, Tarrytown Heights.
REF: CA:94,313; LE:138.

Sugar Loaf Hill
    Captain John Romer used this name in the mid-nineteenth century as an alternate for Kykuit or Davids' Hill.
    REF: MC:850-851.

Suncliff
    Suncliff was the estate of Charles J. Gould. It was located west of Beech Lane and north of Mekeel Avenue. Gould purchased the land from Jacob Storm about 1882.
    See Clear View.
    REF: AR [Apr. 15 1882]; FO:72; M35; M40; M41.

Sunnyside
    This was the estate of American literary great, Washington Irving. Today it is a historic site, operated by Historic Hudson Valley. Sunnyside straddles Sunnyside Brook, which divides Irvington and Tarrytown. The northern portion of the estate is in the Village of Tarrytown, the southern portion is in the Village of Irvington.
    Sunnyside is situated on land which was leased to Wolfert Acker at the turn of seventeenth century. After the Revolution, Philipse Manor was sold and this farm became the property of Jacob Van Tassel, the tenant who had been farming it. He purchased the land on December 8, 1785. Van Tassel had paid an annual rent of three pounds, four shillings and six pence as a tenant of the Manor of Philipsburgh. He also owed Frederick Philipse III about twenty-seven pounds. It was not unusual for Philipse's tenants to have debts of this kind.
    In 1802 the property was sold to Oliver Ferris, and in 1835 to Washington Irving who named it Sunnyside. Irving originally had ten acres, to which he added eight a few years later. The property ultimately included twenty-four acres. The tenant farmhouse was remodeled between 1835 and 1837 in accordance with Irving's instructions. The house was expanded in 1847. Irving called Sunnyside home from 1837 until his death in 1859, although he did live in Spain from 1842 until 1846 while serving as United States minister there.
    After Irving's death in 1859, his nieces continued to live at Sunnyside. In 1896, an Irving relation purchased the place and it remained in the family until 1945. At that time it was obtained by John

Sunnyside
The home of author Washington Irving.
Etching by Lossing.

D. Rockefeller, Jr., and in 1947 [according to TN] the house was opened to the public. By 1961 it had been carefully restored. Today Sunnyside is still open to the public. The house has been furnished and decorated with period furnishings, many of them original. The estate features gardens, an icehouse, a smokehouse, and attractive grounds. Sunnyside is a National Historic Landmark.

See Wolfert's Roost.

VAR: *Sunny Side, Sunnyside Restoration.*
REF: *BA:44,127; BAC:239; BOL:Map; BU:28,32-73; CA:32; CAL2; CON:22,34; CRA:79; DA2:np; DAI:33,36; GE:26; GET:21; HA:106,109-136; HARP:np[pics]; HHV1; HI:17; HUFE:87-88: IN:50; LO:341-352; M1; M29; M39; M58; M60; MI:7[cap]; NE [Aug. 21 1994]; OW:51[cap.]; PHI:np; SC:231; TAP:np; TAR:3; ; TN [May 31 1996 & pic]; WA:15.*

Sunnyside Brook

This brook at Sunnyside which was called Biseghtick by Native Americans empties into the Hudson River.

See Biseghtick.

VAR: *Brook at Sunnyside, Sunnyside brook.*
REF: *HUFE:97; LE:139; M20:22; MI:8[cap],10; SC:231.*

Swan Lake*

This lake is located in the Rockefeller Preserve. It was formed by the damming of Trout Brook in the time of Mrs. John D. Rockefeller, Jr. (Abby Aldrich Rockefeller).

REF: *LE:140; M64; TN [Aug. 2 1996].*

Tappan Hill

The hill shared by Tappan Hill Restaurant and Tappan Hill School has long had this name. It was at one time part of the estate owned by Mark Twain. Canning [CA] relates that the hill was known for its chestnut trees. The name was inspired by the beautiful views of the Tappan Zee, which can be seen from the hilltop.

This was also the name of the residential real estate development organized by developer David Swope and announced on April 4, 1942.

See Halleston, Hillcrest, Tappan Zee.

REF: *CA:232-233; CON:36; DA [Apr. 4 1942, p.1]; DA2 [May 22 1942]; M19; TAR:48.*

Tappan Landing

Tappan Landing is a twentieth century residential development on the site of Glen Mary, the former Lewis estate. The district is located south of Church Street. This land was part of the post-Revolutionary farm of William and James Van Wart.

Tappan Landing was laid out and built under the direction of post-World War II developer, David Swope. [See picture of Swope in TARR.]

See Glen Mary.

REF: *CA:47,235; M1; ST; TA:40; TARR:np[& pic].*

Tappan Zee, the

Washington Irving referred to the Tappan Zee ironically as "the great Mediterranean Sea of the New Netherlands" and claimed that early Dutch sea captains were superstitious about entering these waters [AM]. The Tappan Zee is noted for its beauty, as a fishery, and as a resource for swimming, boating, and windsurfing. All of the Hudson River frontage bordering Sleepy Hollow and Tarrytown lies on the Tappan Zee.

This three-mile-wide bay or widening of the Hudson is named for a tribe of the Delaware group of Native Americans who inhabited the western shore. The Tappans were closely related to the Weckquaesgecks who lived in the area of the villages of Sleepy Hollow, Tarrytown, Irvington, and Dobbs Ferry.

A map of the New Netherlands dating from 1656 labels the "Taappans" as a tribe of American Indians located across the Hudson from Alipconck. This name is said to derive from the Delaware term, *Tup-hanne*, meaning "cold stream."

A map of 1888 depicting the manors of Westchester County, labels a stream entering the Hudson near Nyack as "Tappan Creek." An earlier map (1778) by American cartographer Robert Erskine shows "Tappan Creek" running into the Hudson south of Nyack, near Piermont. Erskine labeled the Hudson at this point the "Tappan Sea," an Anglicization of the Dutch place name. [See also the map in Bolton [BOL] for the position of Tappan Creek.]

VAR: *Tappan Sea, the; Tappan Bay, Topan Sea, Tapan Sea.*

REF: *AM:621; BAC:211; CAL2; CRA:229[& pic]; DA2:np ; DU:3; HAR [Apr. 1876, p. 643]; HI:17; HO:139; IN:51,58; IR:21,297,299,651; IRVI:303; LE:141; LO:325,351-352; LOS:193; M3; M4; M10;*

Tappan Zee
From Pierson Park at the Tarrytown waterfront. Photo by Henry Steiner.

M11; M13; M16; M17; M59; M61; M66; M67; MI:20; MO:26; NE [Aug. 21 1994]; OE:17; OW:51[cap.]; PHI:np; TAP:np; TAR:6; WO:8.

Tappan Zee Bridge

The completed bridge was originally dedicated on December 15, 1955. A ferry operated between Tarrytown and Nyack for many years before the opening of the bridge. About 1995, the Tappan Zee Bridge was renamed, Malcolm Wilson Tappan Zee Bridge, after the former New York State Governor.

See Tappan Zee.
VAR: Malcolm Wilson Tappan Zee Bridge.
REF: CRA:[pics.]; DAI[map]; GM:6-7 & pic; M19; TAP:np; TARR:np.

Tappan Zee Park

This is apparently the name of a place that never existed. The original designers of Philipse Manor intended to leave a park around Centennial Tower, near Philipse Manor Station. This seems never to have occurred.

See Centennial Tower.
REF: CA:47; HU:183.

Tarry Crest

This is the residential area surrounding Crest Drive in the Village of Tarrytown. It lies between Tarry Crest Swimming Club, Highland Avenue, Union Avenue, and Benedict Avenue. The Tarry Crest is commonly referred to as two divisions, the Upper Crest and the Lower Crest. The Lower Crest is that part of the Crest more or less level with Hackley Field; the Upper Crest is the higher ground.

The residences in this neighborhood were developed in the 1940s and the 1950s, largely by David Bogdanoff. A 1937 newspaper refers to "the Tarrytown Crest development" as bordering Benedict Avenue. This appears to be the section which was first developed.
VAR: The Crest, the Tarrytown Crest development.
REF: CA:312; DA2 [May 26 1937]; NE [Aug. 21 1994]; ST; TAR:40; TARR:np & pic.

Tarry Hill

Tarry Hill is a twentieth century residential development east of

Broadway, near the southern border of Tarrytown. The main road is named Tarry Hill Road. In the late nineteenth century this land, directly across Broadway from Lyndhurst, belonged to Jay Gould.
REF: CA:233; M40; WES [FALL 1991,p. 78].

Tarrytown
This name begins to appear in documents at the time of the Revolution. [See the references in AC for two contemporary examples.] How it was derived, or whether it was in use long before this time, is not clear. David Williams, one of the three captors of Major André, stated towards the end of his life, "I was born in Tarrytown then called Philips' Manor, Westchester County, New York, October 21st, 1754." This seems to suggest that the name might have been first used some time after 1754 and before the first written instances of the name appeared in 1775. Of course, this is hardly conclusive.

Raymond [RA:111] gives September 2, 1775, as the date of the earliest record of the name. On this occasion it was used in recording the formation of the Tarrytown Company of the Philipsburgh militia. Captain Abraham Storms was the first captain elected to lead this company. Throughout the Revolution there were frequent recorded references to the name.

Over the years, there has been much discussion of Irving's ironic derivation of this place name in the "Legend of Sleepy Hollow":
> This name was given, we are told, in former days,
> by the good housewives of the adjacent country,
> from the inveterate propensity of their husbands
> to linger about the village tavern on market days.

Some have actually taken the derivation seriously, disparaging Irving's talents as a historian. Irving demonstrated his considerable abilities as a historian and a biographer throughout his career, but his derivation of the name Tarrytown is clearly a joke. It demonstrates his polished irony at its best. Yet even as satire Irving disavows it:
> Be this as it may, I do not vouch for the fact, but
> merely advert to it, for the sake of being precise
> and authentic.

Lederer [LE] writes that the derivation of the name Tarrytown is "debatable." He prefers *Tarwe dorp* or "wheat town."

As mentioned earlier, until 1870 the name Tarrytown applied to

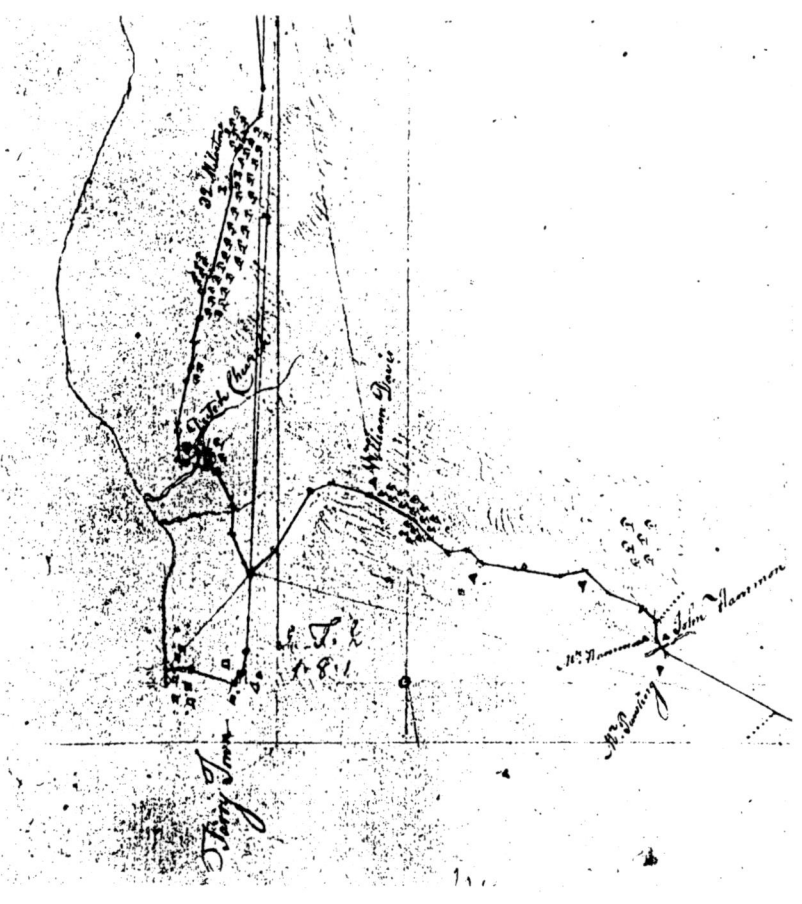

Erskine Survey
Detail [M12] showing Tarrytown & Sleepy Hollow area in the period of the Revolution. Note "S-curve" at Pocantico River crossing. Courtesy New York Historical Society.

a central district or hamlet near Main Street and to an undefined area around it. The name referred to points well outside today's village limits, including areas now in the Village of Sleepy Hollow. This distinction can be confusing, and when we speak of early times in Tarrytown, it is best to differentiate between the early hamlet and the village corporation of 1870. This point is further complicated by the fact that, at least until recently, parts of the Village of Sleepy Hollow (North Tarrytown) were still incorrectly referred to as Tarrytown.

How the hamlet of Tarrytown evolved in pre-Revolutionary times is still a mystery. One would expect to find a settlement of this type developing closer to the Upper Mills where the church and mill were already located. However that area was reserved to the colonial lord-of-the-manor Frederick Philipse III and this fact may have precluded settlement. Whatever caused the hamlet to spring up at the Tarrytown waterfront, it appears that early occupants were engaged in activities which did not require as much land as farming. Some local folk were engaged in tavern or innkeeping (the Van Tassel Tavern, the Couenhoven Inn) and others (like the Requa, Martlings and perhaps the Paulding families) were active in waterfront commerce and the operation of market boats to and from Manhattan. "Daniel Mertlings" paid one pound, five shillings per annum for his "lot," presumably the one near the Tarrytown waterfront.

During and immediately after the Revolution, the hamlet was concentrated near the water at the foot of Main Street. Later, in the early nineteenth century, Irving remarked in one of his letters at how the hamlet had ascended the hill eastward up to the Albany Post Road.

Another question arises with respect to the "Tarrytown Lots." Were these divisions invented upon the sale of Philipsburgh after the Revolution, or did they represent parcels already occupied by Philipsburgh tenants? The answer to this question could help us know the extent to which Tarrytown was developed at the time of the Revolution.

See Tarrytown, Village of and Tarrytown Lots.

VAR: Tarwe-town, Tarwen Dorp, Tarwedurp, Terwe Town, Terrytown, Terry Town, Tarry-Town; Tarry Town.

REF: AC:10,11; CA:16,24; CON:33; DA2 [Dec. 7 1929], [Mar. 12 1937]; DE:3; EA:108; EW:149,157,246,351,358; FE:vol.15, vol.1:304; GR:48; HA:89; HAND:23,30,59; HIN:268,278; HIST:70; HU:30,52; HUF:75; IN:50-58; IR:21,651; IRVIN:108;

HO:140; LE:141; LOS:185; M1; M3; M11; M12; M13; M15; M16; M17; M33[COL:129]; M45; M59; M61; MC:II60- 137; MI:1; OC:[vol.8]735; OW:9; PA:109,115; RA:47,111; RAY:10; RAYM:np.; RO:5; SC:192-194,214; SH:25; SL:map; TA2:5,6; TAR:2,4; TR:np; TWO:47; WO:31[map].

Tarrytown, Village of

The Village of Tarrytown, incorporated in 1870, includes all or most of the historic settlement or hamlet named Tarrytown. In the north, the village line was drawn along the town line of Greenburgh. A good deal of this border is traced by André Brook.

In the south the village extends to Sunnyside Brook, in the west to the Hudson River, and eastward to just past Midland Avenue. (The Lower Lake, also in the village, extends more eastward yet.)

See Tarrytown.

REF: M21; M49; SH:611,619.

Tarrytown Bay

This was literally the wide shallow bay which stood at the foot of Franklin Street in the mid-nineteenth century. Over time it has been filled in and developed. Depot Plaza now occupies the place where Tarrytown Bay once lay.

The bay was partially formed by Tarrytown Point and Holmes Point. Between them was the mouth of André Brook. Silting of the harbor was accelerated by the construction of the Hudson River Rail Road bed in the mid-nineteenth century.

See Martling's Landing and Tarrytown Point.

REF: M51.

Tarrytown Cemetery

Sleepy Hollow Cemetery was organized under this name on October 27, 1849. On February 9, 1865, it was renamed Sleepy Hollow Cemetery. It appears that even after the renaming of the cemetery, it retained a portion of the old name. The cemetery is still advertised as "Sleepy Hollow Cemetery at Tarrytown." See the discussions of "Tarrytown" and "Tarrytown, Village of" for some explanation of the rationale behind this.

See Sleepy Hollow Cemetery.

VAR: *Tarrytown cemetery.*

REF: CA:309 ; COLL:30; JE:384; LOS:191; M2; MI:9; WEST:734-735.

Tarrytown Harbor
   Surveyor William Adams used this name for Tarrytown Bay in his township map of Greenburgh, about 1797. See Tarrytown Bay. *CA:273; M31.*

Tarrytown Heights [Tarrytown]
   This name was used more frequently in former times to designate the high ground between Wilson Park and Hackley School. It appears that in the early twentieth century, the station on the New York & Northern line, which had formerly been named Tarrytown, eventually was called Tarrytown Heights. This was possibly to differentiate it from the Tarrytown Station by the Hudson River. In 1926, a map [M29] showed Tarrytown Heights as the railroad station located at what is now the Tarrytown Lakes skating dock.
   At one time the name Tarrytown Heights applied also to Pocantico Hills and Pocantico Hills Station. For this reason it is possible to mistake one place for the other. The Tarrytown Heights depot was located at the bottom of Sunnyside Avenue, and the place name seems to have included Union Avenue and beyond. Canning [CA:136] seems to consider Tarrytown Heights as including the ridge running along Marymount Avenue. Lederer [LE] defines this place as the area "east of Castle Ridge and south of the lakes...." A community guide of the 1950s makes a distinction between "the Heights" and Tarry Crest.
   See Tarrytown Heights* [Pocantico Hills].
VAR: The Heights.
REF: AB:[map]; CA:56,136,193,312-313; CON:21,40; DA2 [Sept. 28 1932]; HISTOR:np; HUT:157; LE:141; M29; OW:23,29; RA:99; TA:map; TAR:40; TARR:np.

Tarrytown Heights* [Pocantico Hills]
   Tarrytown Heights was formerly the name of the hamlet atop the western slope of Buttermilk Hill, today known as Pocantico Hills. This area was mainly farmland prior to 1860. In the 1870s [See M65] and early 1880s, the Tarrytown Land Company planned to use this name for the future development of what was to be Pocantico Hills, but the company had financial difficulties and the scheme was dropped.

At that time Tarrytown Heights was a growing community of about 150 people. This place was to become the unincorporated hamlet of Pocantico Hills.
See Pocantico Hills, and Tarrytown Heights [Tarrytown].
VAR: The Heights.
REF: HUFE:98; LE:141; M36; M65; MI:9,18,20,21; PO:148,154; SC:206,285,305; WEST:730.

Tarrytown High Pressure Reservoir
See Tarrytown Lakes.
VAR: Tarrytown Reservoir.
REF: LE:141, M7.

Tarrytown Lakes, the
This name refers to the Upper and the Lower Lakes together. They were created by the damming of Storm Brook. According to the Tarrytown Centennial Album [TARR], two wells were established in the Storm Brook Valley about 1887. The two islands in the Lower Lake are vestiges of this construction. Subsequently, in 1888, the reservoir was created.
Today the reservoirs still deliver part of Tarrytown's water supply. They are also an excellent recreational resource for residents and visitors. The Lakes and neighboring trails afford opportunities for fishing, jogging, biking, walking, roller-blading, and enjoying nature. In cold winters the Upper Lake is open for skating.
See Lower Lake, Upper Lake, Storm Brook.
VAR: Tarrytown Reservoir.
REF: DA2 [May 22 1942]; HU:36; LE:138,141; M19; M20:23; M47; M58; NE [Aug. 21 1994]; RO:np; TAR,45; TARR:np; TN [Aug. 2 1996].

Tarrytown Landing
Raymond [RA:183] describes Revolutionary soldier Lt. Richard Peacock of Tarrytown as living "...under the hill at Tarrytown landing, adjoining Widow Martling...."
See Martlings Landing.
REF: M34; RA:183.

Tarrytown Lighthouse, the
In the mid-nineteenth century, a lighthouse was authorized by Congress for Tarrytown Point. After much delay and disagreement

over the proper placement of the structure, a lighthouse was built further north, off the tip of Kingsland Point. Built in 1883, it stands in the waters of the Village of Sleepy Hollow, not Tarrytown. A photograph in TN shows that in the 1930s the mainland was much more distant from the lighthouse. Soon landfilling at the General Motors site was to bring the shoreline much closer to the lighthouse island.

The reason the light was named Tarrytown Lighthouse despite its Sleepy Hollow (North Tarrytown) location may be due to the fact that it was originally projected for Tarrytown. "North Tarrytown" was also a relatively new name when the lighthouse was built.

The lighthouse was commissioned in 1883 and decommissioned in 1965. It had been electrified in the 1940s, but navigational lights on the Tappan Zee Bridge made an operating lighthouse unnecessary. The Tarrytown Lighthouse was purchased by Westchester County in September 1974, and it is open to the public during specially scheduled guided tours.

It appears that an early lighthouse may have preceded the Tarrytown Lighthouse at the tip of Kingsland Point. Howat [HO] writes that a lighthouse is pictured in an 1876 scene of this portion of the Tappan Zee by artist Francis A. Silva. Whether the painting actually depicts the scene he suggests, is not clear.

See Kingsland Point.

VAR: *Tarrytown Light, Kingsland Point lighthouse, Kingsland Point Lighthouse, Lighthouse.*
REF: *BAC:218[pic]; CA:190-192; CAL1[pic]; DAI:33,31; GE:21; GET:24; GM:7 & pic; GR:48; HISTOR:np; HO:139 & [plate 16]; MI:7; M29; MO:17,19[pic]; PEO:69-71; TARR:np; TN [Nov. 29 1996], [June 21 1996 & pic], [June 7 1996 & pic], [Dec. 16 1995 & pic].*

Tarrytown Loop, the

The Tarrytown Loop was also known as the Horseshoe Curve. In November 1881, the New York City and Northern Railroad opened its altered route from Elmsford to Tarrytown Heights [Pocantico Hills]. The new route, known as the Tarrytown Loop, swept along the south and west edges of what was to become the Tarrytown Lakes. There was a station at the southern end of the Lakes known as Tarrytown Heights Station and one at Tower Hill Road known as

Sleepy Hollow Station. The next stop on the line was Tarrytown Heights [Pocantico Hills].
    See the Tarrytown Lakes.
VAR: the Tarrytown *"loup"*, the Horseshoe Curve.
REF: CA:194; HU:156; SC:305.

Tarrytown Lots, the
    A cluster of twenty parcels of land between Main Street and Franklin Street were known as the Tarrytown Lots. Twelve of them were numbered and laid out in 1784. The Tarrytown Lots extended from Requa's Dock to the old Albany Post Road (Broadway).
    These parcels appear on Couzens' map [M1]. For a detailed itemization of the lots and a record of their early owners, please see SC:232. Lot number one, at the corner of Main Street and Broadway, was originally owned by George Combs, who soon sold the lot and house to Revolutionary war hero John Dean. Dean started a post office and general store in the place. The store was later called "Tommy Dean's" after John Dean's son, who continued the family business. Washington Irving and his nieces were regular patrons of Thomas Dean's store. [See Dean Park.]
    Irving wrote about the early development of Tarrytown in 1839:
> The spirit of speculation and improvement had seized even upon that once quiet and unambitious little dorp. The whole neighborhood was laid out into town lots. Instead of the little tavern below the hill, where the farmers used to loiter on market days, and indulge in cider and gingerbread, an ambitious hotel, with cupola and verandahs, now crested the summit, among churches built in the Grecian and Gothic styles, showing a great increase in piety and polite taste in the neighborhood.

    Here Irving is writing that the early focus of activity in the hamlet was near the waterfront at a tavern presumably run by the Requas or the Martlings. Further on in the piece, he appears to be alluding to the Martin Smith Inn which at a later time "crested the summit." This inn, at the northwest corner of Main and Broadway, was the successor of the Edward Couenhoven Inn. Irving does not seem to be aware of the fact that the lots had been drawn up fifteen

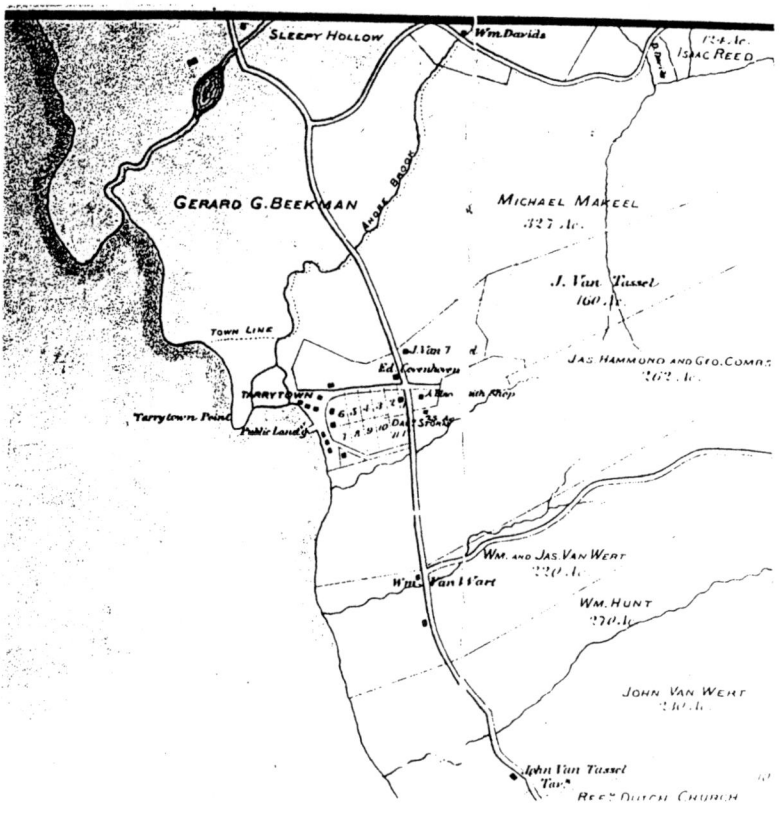

Couzins Map
Detail [M1] showing the outlines of Pocantico Bay (Slapershaven), Sleepy Hollow, Pugsley's Point, Tarrytown Point, Tarrytown Bay, the Tarrytown Lots, etc. Courtesy New York Public Library.

years before he first visited Tarrytown as a youth. It seems that little had been done with most of the parcels in those early years.
See Tarrytown.
REF: IRVING:13; M1; SC:232.

Tarrytown Point
Tarrytown Point is at the west end of Main Street. Today it is not much of a point, but it was more pronounced before the filling in of Tarrytown Bay to create more real estate. On Couzens map (M1), the point can been seen on the north side of the mouth of André Brook. Adams' map [M31] is an excellent source for the configuration of the point and bay in post-Revolutionary times. Tarrytown Point is really the "point" referred to in the name Point Landing. It was the site originally intended for the Tarrytown Lighthouse, which may explain the lighthouse's misnomer.
See Point Landing and Tarrytown Lighthouse.
REF: CA:190, M1; M6; M31.

Tarrytown Railroad Station
According to MO, the first New York Central train went through the Tarrytowns in 1850. The first wooden station house was built in 1850 by Seth Bird. It stood about one hundred yards north of the present station. A later station was built in 1870, and the current one was constructed in 1890.
The Tarrytown Heights Railroad Station was also known by this name.
See Northern Depot and Tarrytown Heights [Tarrytown].
REF: CAL1; CH:Summer,1994(No.22); M40; TAR:37.

Tarrytowns, the
The villages of Sleepy Hollow (formerly North Tarrytown) and Tarrytown together are known as the Tarrytowns. Many influences from early times, such as family ties, intermarriages, and topography, have given the inhabitants of both villages the sense of living in one community. This cultural connection has survived major political events. One such event was the creation of post-Revolutionary townships in 1788. This caused a major boundary line to be drawn through the community along André Brook. The line separated the Township of Mount Pleasant from that of Greenburgh. Yet the community spirit which overreaches the border remained.

This early event set the stage for a more profound separation. In 1870, a new state law made it advantageous for the larger hamlets to incorporate as villages. As a result, the villages of Tarrytown and Sleepy Hollow (North Tarrytown) were created, with separate governments, schools, fire departments, and services. The two halves of the community were now not only in different townships, but separate village corporations with their own governments. This presented an additional challenge to a united community spirit. The separation of these two newly defined incorporated villages was intensified by attendant competition in industry, local commerce, and even school rivalries.

Nevertheless, a sense of common interest and traditional neighborliness has preserved the connection between the two villages. In modern times, the separate school systems have merged, which means that public school children routinely reside in one village and attend school in the other. Churches and civic groups commonly draw their members from both villages. The two villages share athletic leagues and a historical society. Scharf used the name, "the Tarrytowns," in 1886, commenting that the two villages "are really one." The term is also used in Conklin (1939).

In 1931 and 1932 local newspaper articles reported that a consolidation of the villages was being seriously considered, at least by some parties. There was debate over what the merged municipality would be called. The North Tarrytown Board of Trustees favored the name Fremont, others liked Tarrytown. In a previous vote on consolidation in 1916, Tarrytown had voted against a merger by a margin of 71 votes, while the measure had been approved in North Tarrytown by a margin of 82 votes. The idea of merging the two villages continues to be raised from time to time.

VAR: The two Tarrytowns.
REF: CA:304; CON:np,7; DA2 [Sept. 28 1932], [May 27 1942]; DAI:31; GE:2; GET:5; HU:153; MI:1; MO:10,33; NORT:3; PHI:np; SC:195; ST; TAR:1; TW:22; YE:np;

Tower Hill

Sleepy Hollow Railroad Station was later known as Tower Hill Station. The station stop on the New York and Northern Railway appears on a map of 1893. It continued in use during the first three decades of the twentieth century. (See train schedules reproduced in

HUT.) The station was located on the County House Road (also called Tower Hill Road) near the west side of the Lower Lake. The old railroad bed can still be found in the surrounding woods, and joggers use it frequently.

The station was named for the hill which the track then ascended to the north; the hill was named for the tower which a property owner had built on the hill. According to Lederer [LE:144], John D. Rockefeller's predecessor on this portion of Kykuit Hill, Wilson H. Blackwell, built a lookout tower which the public was free to visit. The tower was located on the east side of Kykuit, north of the Lower Lake.

See Sleepy Hollow Railroad Station.

REF: CA:194; LE:144; M41; OW:23; HUT:85,157; ST; HISTOR:np; M29; TARR:np [& pic].

Underhill

This is the area at the foot of Franklin and Main Streets. Ironically, it was in this district that Sergeant Isaac Martlings was murdered by Nathaniel Underhill on May 26, 1779. After the war Underhill immigrated to Nova Scotia along with many other Loyalists.

In Raymond [RA] (1894), Revolutionary War soldier Joseph Paine of Tarrytown is said to have lived "...under the hill and near Martlings Landing...." In 1840, Washington Irving wrote to his sister, "When you knew the village [Tarrytown], it was little better than a mere hamlet, crouched down at the foot of a hill, with its dock for the accommodation of the weekly market sloop."

The term later applied to the Orchard Street business district. An association of merchants there was known as the Underhill Merchants Association.

VAR: the hill, under the hill.
REF: BU:30; CA:36,277; COLL:14; DA2 [Sept. 28 1932], [July 11 1933]; EA:110; RA:182, 183; RO:5; TAR:48.

Upper Crest, the

See the Crest, and Tarry Crest.
REF: ST.

Upper Dock

About 1835, three to five sloops sailed weekly to New York

from this dock at the foot of Beekman Avenue. The name is appears on a map of 1851.
See Beekman Town Landing, Martling's Landing, North Landing.
REF: M2; SC:287.

Upper Lake, the
The Upper Lake is the smaller and more southerly of the two Tarrytown Lakes; its waters trickle into the Lower Lake. The southern end of the Upper Lake is occasionally used for ice skating.
VAR: Upper Reservoir, the.
REF: CA:136; M20:23; M45; M47; M58; TAR:22.

Upper Mills, the
This is how Frederick Philipse I styled his northern milling establishment. The Lower Mills was located next to the manor house at Yonkers, beside the Saw Mill River. The Upper Mills was built on the Pocantico River, at the site of what is today known as the Philipsburg Manor Restoration–Upper Mills. Some suggest that there might have been a mill on the site before that of Frederick Philipse I.

The mill was established by Philipse about 1685. Lederer [LE] notes that the Upper Mills was established about 1682. A booklet published by Sleepy Hollow Restorations [PHILI] suggests that Philipse had been granted rights to construct a mill as early as 1680 and that its construction began immediately. In the days of Philipsburgh, the term Upper Mills referred to the area near the mill, including the house, barn, dam, surrounding fields, forests, and possibly the church.

Adolphus Philipse inherited this portion of the manor from his father when he inherited all of Upper Philipsburgh. By the time of Adolphus's death in 1750, there were twenty-three slaves at the Upper Mills. At that time his portion of the manor reverted to his nephew, Frederick Philipse II. Frederick died a year later, leaving all of Philipsburgh to his son, Frederick Philipse III. In 1761, the new "lord" made a thirty-one-year lease of the property to William Pugsley, which carried a restriction on the amount of lumber Pugsley could cut from forest lands. The Pugsley lease included 720 acres.

According to Conklin [CON:19], the original mill was removed near the turn of the twentieth century. She writes that a man named

Conover was the last to own and operate the mill. This seems to conflict with other sources.

See Pugsley's Point.

VAR: Upper Plantation, Phillips Upper Mills, Upper Mills; upper mills; the Philipse Mills.

REF: CA:26,139; COLL:3; DE:4; FE:vol.15,vol.1:303-304; FI:np; GE:11; HA:27,65; HO:140; HU:10; JE:381; KE:231; LE:148; Ml1; MO:4; OW:12,14; P4; PHIL:np; PHILI:23,26,29-55; SH:162; TAR:1,2; TN [Oct. 31 1996]; VAND:[map]; WIL:[pic].

Upper Philipsburgh

This is the portion of Philipsburgh Manor extending from Dobbs Ferry northwards. After the death of Frederick Philipse I, his manor was divided between his son Adolphus and his grandson Frederick II. Lower Philipsburgh was inherited by Frederick II; this included lands in the modern municipalities of Yonkers and possibly Hastings-on-Hudson.

Upper Philipsburgh went to Adolphus. It included most of the lands between Dobbs Ferry and the Croton River. Muster rolls from the time of the Revolution list militia companies from Upper Philipsburgh, East Philipsburgh, and Lower Philipsburgh as well as a Tarrytown company. An unfootnoted passage in Oechsner's, *Ossining, New York, An Informal Bicentennial History* [OE] mentions that, in 1742, Philipsburgh was subdivided into eleven "small manors." This might help to explain the names of the various militia companies and the emergence of the name Tarrytown.

See Philipsburgh.

VAR: Upper Philipseburgh Manor.

REF: FER:303-304; SH:226-227; TWO:122,132.

Van Tassel Tavern

See Jacob Mott House.

Veruselle

Veruselle was the eighty-eight-acre estate of Russell Hopkins in southern Tarrytown. He purchased the place in 1909 and began a kind of private zoo on his land. It appears that the estate was named for his wife Vera. See Canning [CA] for a detailed description of the estate and an account of Hopkins.

See The Lindens.
REF: CA:228-229.

Wackandeco

This, along with several other variations, is a rendering of the name "Pocantico" in the Royal Charter of Philipsburgh, 1693.

See Pocantico.

VAR: *Weghkandeco, Pugkanteko, Puegkandico.*
REF: BOL:vol.II,591,592.

Waldheim

Waldheim was the former estate of New York City born William H. Webb (1816-1888), a noted shipbuilder. Waldheim is shown in a map of 1891 as an eighty-two-acre estate. It lay west of today's Midland Avenue and north of Benedict Avenue. Waldheim's lands were formerly part of the William and James Van Wert farm (230 acres), as were all the lands directly west to Holmes Point.

Webb purchased the land in 1882 from John S. Mitchell. He refurbished the house and, according to a contemporary newspaper account, expanded the estate to one hundred acres by the time of his death.

Hackley School, established in 1899, is now largely situated on this land.

See Hackley Hill.

REF: *AR [Sept. 8 1888]; M35; M40; MI:21; SC: 232,245,248[pic]; TA:map.*

Washington Irving Memorial Bridge

See Sleepy Hollow Bridge, Headless Horseman Bridge.

REF: *DA [Sept. 28, 1914, p.1]; DA2 [Dec. 31 1930]; RO:22.*

Washington Square

This was a name for the square at the junction of Valley, Washington, and Chestnut Streets in the 1880s. It was officially renamed Robertson Square in 1959.

See Robertson Square.

REF: HU:116,152.

Webber Park
This 1926 residential development is named for John Webber, a Sleepy Hollow (North Tarrytown) village attorney. When John Anderson died in 1880, Webber became an executor of his estate. In 1886, Webber purchased the Anderson property. Webber Park lies, roughly speaking, between Broadway and New Broadway.
See Anderson Park, Sleepy Hollow Park, Irving Park.
REF: *CA:40,289; HU:88,155; LE:153; M41; MO:7; TAR:40.*

Weckquaesgeck
This name means "the place of the bark kettle." It was an early Delaware Indian name for the lands about the Tarrytowns, Irvington, and Dobbs Ferry. The name also applies to the Delaware tribe which lived there. Some forms of the name also apply to Wickers Creek, the stream which connects with the Hudson near the northern border of Dobbs Ferry. In "Wolfert's Roost," Irving mentioned that the tribal lands of these Indians extended from "...Yonkers quite to Sleepy Hollow...."

In February 1624, a contemporary commentator named Nicholaes Van Wassenaer [JA] notes:
> Below the Maikans [Mohicans] are situate these tribes: Mechkentowoon, Tapants [Tappans], on the east side; Wiekajock, Wyeck [Weckquaesgeck], on the east side.

An early Dutch businessman named David De Vries [JA] writes in April 1640:
> Opposite Tapaen lies a place called Wickquaesgeck, where there is a maize-land [cornfields], but all stoney or sandy, and where many pine trees grow. We generally haul pine masts from there. The land is also mountainous.

In 1642 he again writes:
> I will state something of the nations about Fort Amsterdam; as the Hackinsack, Tapaen, and Wicquaesgeck Indians; and these are located at some two, three, or four leagues from the entrance of the [Hudson] river.

An anonymous reporter of the same period [JA] writes in 1642 that:

> ...he [an Indian] of Witqueshreeck living northeast of Manhatans, perpetrated another murderous deed in the house of an old man....

He writes again in 1642:

> Meanwhile God wreaked vengeance on those of Witquescheck without our knowledge through the Mahicanders dwelling below Fort Orange, who slew seventeen of them, and made prisoners of many women and children.

In 1644 he writes:

> The old Indian captured above having promised to lead us to Wetquescheck, which consisted of three castles, sixty-five men were despatched under Baxter and Pieter Cock, who found them empty, though thirty Indians could have stood against two hundred soldiers since the castles were constructed of plank five inches thick, nine feet high, and braced around with thick balk full of port-holes. Our people burnt two, reserving the third for a retreat.

VAR: *Wickquaesgeck, Wecquaes-Keck, Wiechquaeskeck, Wicquaeskeck, Wiekagjock, Wicquas-geck, Witqueshreeck, Witquescheck, Wetquescheck, Wickquaesquick, Weekersqueeke, Wysquaqua, William Portugues creek, Wickers Creek, Wiquaskeek, Weghquegsik, Wegquiskeek, Wegqueskeek, Weckquakeek.*

REF: *BOL:vol.I,274-275; BOL:vol.II,592-593; FE:276; HA:25; HAD1:37; IR:299; JA:67,206,216,274-277,281; OC:[vol.5]365,366; OCA:366; TA:6; TWO:47.*

Westchester County

The Town of Westchester was elevated to the status of a "borough" in 1696. It was located in what is now the Bronx. Borough status was a distinction shared with only one other community in the colonial Province of New York. The honor may have been partially due to its distinction as the first English settlement in the county. The status may also have been conferred in consideration of the settlement's size and its proximity to Manhattan. Patented as a town in 1667, it was designated the county seat when the Province of New York was divided into counties in 1683.

The County of Westchester was named for its county seat, the Town of Westchester. The town became part of the Bronx in the 1873-74 annexation of that area by New York City. Before that time, the county's southern limit extended all the way to the southern border of the Bronx.

In 1758 the county courthouse at Westchester burned down and a new one was constructed at White Plains, which then became the new county seat, possibly due to the fact that it was centrally located.
VAR: West Chester.
REF: FI:5; LOS:185; M4; SH:197-198,227.

Widow Beekman's Farm
See Beekman Farm.
REF: PE1: vol.24/3 328.

Wildey's Swamp
This swamp was part of the lands owned by Caleb Wildey. It bordered André Brook on the west side of Broadway. Today the area is called Patriots Park. Lossing [LOS] refers to it in the mid-nineteenth century: "The marshy and thickly-wooded glen into which it [André Brook] poured was known as Wiley's Swamp."
See Clark's Kill and Patriots Park.
VAR: Wiley's Swamp [M17].
REF: CA:202; IRVI:327; HIST:179-180; LOS:185; M17; M57; YE:np.

Willow Brook
Willow Brook was formerly the estate of Edward S. Jaffray, a successful dry-goods merchant of New York. The place was located east of Sunnyside and north of Sunnyside Lane, where Shadow Brook lies today. Jaffray purchased this estate from Ambrose Kingsland in 1854.
VAR: Willowbrook.
REF: CA:56; SC:239.

Wilson Park
This is a residential area named for William S. Wilson; it includes the land near and adjoining Wilson Park Drive. Wilson had approximately twenty acres with an orchard and a vineyard. Wilson Park, however, refers to a larger area extending from County House

Road (Tower Hill Road) to Mekeel Avenue. The land was part of the property which Mikel Mekeel sold earlier to his son-in-law, Caleb Wildey. Wildey afterwards sold the land to his own son-in-law, Captain Jacob Storm.

The well-known American artist, Rockwell Kent (b. 1882), was born in Wilson Park and lived there for a time.

See Pleasance, Suncliff and Storm Brook.

REF: *CA:105,202,237; CON:36; DA2 [Mar. 12 1937]; HIS:40; LE:addenda; M40; M41; NE [Aug. 21 1994]; TAR:40.*

Windle Park

Windle Park was named for a Mr. Windle of Windle and Crocker, a company which began the development of this area. Starr's Military Academy moved to the Windle Park area in Tarrytown after having been located in Sleepy Hollow (North Tarrytown). It remained until the 1890s, and subsequently a school for girls occupied the building. After that, the Windlemere Inn did business in the same structure. The area is now mainly residential, overlooking Depot Plaza and the Tarrytown waterfront. The Tarrytown YMCA is in this district.

REF: *CA:161,203; DA2 [Apr. 19 1937], [Nov. 11 1942], [Feb. 17 1943 & pic].*

Wolf Hill

Wolf Hill is the hill south of Prospect Avenue. Overlooking the Tappan Zee, it is said to be where Washington first observed British warships ascending the Hudson in the summer of 1776. We can only guess why it was called Wolf Hill.

See the Sigafus Estate, Pine Tree Lot, Edgemont.

REF: *CA:237; RAY:11.*

Wolfert's Dell

Moses Hicks Grinnell [1803-1877] was a wealthy New York merchant and an influential politician. He was related by marriage to Washington Irving, and the place name is probably derived from Wolfert's Roost. Grinnell's estate was located on the Hudson River, south of Lyndhurst and north of Willow Brook. A reference cited in Scharf [SC] suggests that he may have been instrumental in obtaining Irving's appointment as minister to Spain.

Wolfert's Roost
A Philipsburgh Manor tenant farmhouse,
later Sunnyside Etching by Lossing.

Grinnell and his brothers had publishing interests in New York. They helped to finance some of the earliest Arctic expeditions. Grinnell served as a Whig Party representative to Congress, as a presidential elector on the Frémont ticket in 1856, and as president of the Union League from 1867-1873. His friends included Daniel Webster and William H. Seward.

During the 1880s and 1890s, the estate was owned by James H. Banker and subsequently by Banker's widow, Mrs. Ellen J. Banker. The Grinnell house stood until the 1960s when a fire destroyed most of the structure.

REF: AP M40; SC:241; ZU:80.

Wolfert's Roost

According to Washington Irving, Sunnyside was known by this name during the tenure of early colonial settler Wolfert Acker. Whether Irving was in earnest is difficult to determine. He writes that the place name is an English corruption of the Dutch, *Wolfert's Rust*, which translates, "Wolfert's Rest."

Irving writes that the earliest colonist named Wolfert Acker served on the council of Peter Stuyvesant after arriving in New Amsterdam from Holland. When the British took New York from the Dutch, he was said to have sought retirement at this homestead by the banks of the Hudson. Wolfert Ecker (Acker) is listed as a deacon and elder of the Old Dutch Church of Sleepy Hollow in the year 1697 [FI].

A Wolfert Acker of Revolutionary times was a member of the New York State Committee of Public Safety in 1776. The rent he was required to pay as a tenant of Frederick Philipse III appears to have been two pounds. But this may have applied to a different farm since according to Irving, the "Roost" was in the hands of Jacob Van Tassel by the time of the Revolution.

See Sunnyside.

VAR: Wolfert's Rust *(Wolfert's Rest)*, the Roost.
REF: BA:44,136; BAC:217; CON:34; DA2 *[Mar. 12 1937]*; FI:9; EA:106; HIN:266,267; HIS:7,13; HU:48; HUT:35,52; IN:50; IR:301; LO:350-351; M57 RO:32; TAP:np.

Yellow Rocks

The writer has found only two published instances of the name, and they are separated by a ninety year gulf. Bacon's [BAC]

1907 reference to the place name "Yellow Rocks" appears to be the earliest in print. This illustrates how inadequate the written record can be as a source for certain place names. Occurrences abound in verbal usage, particularly among fishermen and Sleepy Hollow village "old-timers." Some names plainly enjoy a vigorous life off the printed page.

Yellow Rocks is a point of low, yellowish rocks jutting into the Hudson River at the base of a steep hill north of Philipse Manor Station and south of the *Hafentje*. It is a well-known place for catching striped bass. How long have the bass and the bass fishermen been coming there? It is interesting to speculate that Native Americans might have fished this spot successfully for centuries before the arrival of the first European traders and settlers.

One can still prowl the riverbank at this point and discover the white striations of early oyster "kitchens" (deposits). In May, expectant fishermen stand on the rocks, hoping to take a twenty-pound striped bass as the fish make their spring run north. Village "old-timers" still mention the Yellow Rocks as a summer hangout—a place to go "skinny-dipping" and engage in the time-honored rites of adolescence.
REF: BAC:241; ST; TN [Mar. 30 1996].

Youngs Corners*

The house of Revolutionary figure Joseph Youngs was located at the corner of the Lower Cross Road and the Unionville Road. Today this is the intersection of Route 100C and the Sprain Brook Parkway. Youngs Corners was the site of "the affair at Youngs House" on February 3, 1780.

Youngs was a Revolutionary soldier and a member of the New York Committee of Safety. His son, Samuel, was a "Westchester Guide." Samuel was a young man at the time of the Revolution, and he lived to be an important reporter of the local events of that period. Joseph was a pre-war tenant of Frederick Philipse III, and, for the record, he owed the landlord thirty pounds, three pence on a loan at the time of the war, according to the landlord's calculations.

Through much of the war, the Youngs' house was used as an outpost by the local militia and by regular troops of "the lines." "The lines" was a defensive front which extended roughly between the Tarrytown area and White Plains; it varied north and south as American fortunes fluctuated in this region. Colonel Aaron Burr was one of the more successful commanders of "the lines." Unfortunately, the tenure of his successor, Lieutenant Colonel Thompson, was particularly disastrous. Nearly half of Thompson's command of 250 men were killed or captured at Youngs Corners on February 3, 1780.

The Youngs place was 152 acres in extent according to Lederer [LE]. Youngs bought his tenant farm after the Revolution, and it was subsequently sold to Isaac Van Wart, one of the captors of Major André. Van Wart's son, a minister, inherited the farm and would frequently plow up the skeletal remains of the combatants who had died there. In the early twentieth century, a monument was erected by the roadside over these remains. It commemorates the "Action at Youngs" and the American and British soldiers who were killed there.

See the Four Corners, The Burnt House. See Scharf for more.

VAR: *Young's Corner, Youngs' Corners, Young Corners, Youngs Tavern, Youngs's House, Youngs' Burnt House, Youngs' house, Young's, The Van Wart House.*
REF: AB:87; COLL:16; DE:4; EA:117; HAD2:60; HIN:274; HUF:255,256,324-326,328,381; HUFE:132; HUT:36-39; LE:161; RAYM:np; SC:312; SH:461; TAR:2; YE:np.

Zaag Kill*

The colonial Dutch used this name for the Saw Mill River. The name can be found in seventeenth-century land grants and in Van der Donck's, *A Description of New Netherlands* [VAN].

See Saw Mill River and theNeperhan.
REF: LE:161; VAN:8.

BIBLIOGRAPHY

CODE	SOURCE
AB	Abbott, William. *The Crisis of the Revolution.* Harrison, New York: Harbor Hill Books, 1976. [Reprint. Original edition, 1899.]
ABB	Abbott, William. *The Crisis of the Revolution, Being the Story of Arnold & André.* Illustrations and original photographs by Edwin S. Bennett, issued under the auspices of the Empire State Society, Sons of the American Revolution. New York: William Abbott, 1899. [First edition of 250 copies, pp. 119, in the Greenburgh Library].
AC	*An Account of the Action at Tarrytown and of its Commemoration by the Sons of the Revolution of Tarrytown on July Fifteenth, 1899.* Tarrytown, New York: The Winthrop Press, 1899. [Map, "Tarwe-town in the Manor of Phillipsburgh, Westchester Co. N.Y. 1781. Committee on Publication: Richard B. Coutant, Marcius D. Raymond, George C. Andrews.]
AL	Allport, Susan. *Sermons in Stone.* Illustrated by David Howell. New York: W. W. Norton, 1990.
AM	*A Guide to the Empire State.* American Guide Series, Illustrated. New York: Oxford University Press, 1940.
AN	Anonymous. *Letters about the Hudson River and its Vicinity Written in 1835-1837.* Third edition with additions and engravings. New York: Freeman Hunt and Company, No. 141 Nassau Street, 1837. [A facsimile reprint by J. C. & A. L. Fawcett of the original book.]
AN2	Anonymous. *The Old Dutch Burying Ground of Sleepy Hollow in North Tarrytown, New York. A Record of the Early Gravestones and their Inscriptions, 1953.* Privately printed under the direction of William Graves Perry, Boston, MA. Boston: The Rand Press, 1953.

AND	Anderson, Nancy K. and Linda S. Ferber. *Albert Bierstadt, Art and Enterprise.* New York: Hudson Hills Press, 1990.
AP	*Appleton's Cyclopedia of American Biography.* Edited by James Grant Wilson and John Fiske, VII vols. Detroit: Gale Research Co., 1968. [Originally published, New York: D. Appleton and Company, 1888.]
AR	*Tarrytown Argus.* [1875-1910.]
AT	Atterbury, Henry. Director of Parks and Recreation, Village of Sleepy Hollow. Interview, 1995.
BA	Bacon, Edgar Mayhew. *Chronicles of Tarrytown and Sleepy Hollow.* Third impression. New York and London: G. P. Putnam's Sons, The Knickerbocker Press, 1900. [Originally published in 1897.]
BAC	Bacon, Edgar Mayhew. *The Hudson River From Ocean to Source.* New York and London: G. P. Putnam's Sons, The Knickerbocker Press, 1907.
BACO	Bacon, Edgar Mayhew. *The Capture of Major André, or the Miracle of the Neutral Ground.* n.p.: n.p., n.d. [Written for publication during the sesquicentennial of the Capture, observed in the Tarrytowns in September, 1930. A dramatic sketch followed by a historical article on the capture. Copyright by Edgar Mayhew Bacon, September 1930.]
BAS	Basher, Thomas. Tarrytown village trustee and son of the late Thomas Basher, Sr., former Tarrytown village trustee. Personal communication.
BI	"Bi-Centennial Bus Tour Town of Mount Pleasant, May 14, 1988." Pamphlet. n.p.: n.p., n.d.
BO	Bolton, Robert. *A History of the County of Westchester from the First Settlement to the Present Time.* 2 vols. New York: Alexander S. Gould, 1848.
BOL	Bolton, Robert. *The History of the Several Towns, Manors, and Patents of the County of Westchester.* Edited by the Rev. C. W. Bolton. 2 vols. New York: Chas. F. Roper, 1881.
BU	Butler, Joseph T. *Washington Irving's Sunnyside.* Tarrytown, NY: Sleepy Hollow Restorations, 1974.
CA	Canning, Jeff and Wally Buxton (William C. Gross). *History of the Tarrytowns.* Harrison, New York: Harbor Hill Books, 1975 [Second printing 1988.]

CAL1	"Historical Views of The Tarrytowns, 1987 Calendar." n.p.: n.p., n.d. [Historical Society of The Tarrytowns.]
CAL2	"1996 Sleepy Hollow Country Calendar." [Sleepy Hollow Chamber of Commerce, Tarrytown, NY.]
CAS	*Cassell's English Dutch Dutch English Dictionary.* New York: MacMillan Publishing Company, 1978.
CAST	"The Castle at Tarrytown, A Luxury Inn." [Black & white brochure, two panels, two sides, first distributed in 1996.] n.p.: n.p., n.d.
CE	Ceconi, Giovanna. Personal communication.
CEC	Ceconi, Walter. Personal communication.
CH	*The Chronicle.* Periodical of the Historical Society of the Tarrytowns.
COL	Colles, Christopher. *A Survey of the Roads of the United States of America, 1789.* Walter W. Ristow, ed. Cambridge, Massachusetts: The Belnap Press of Harvard University Press, 1961.
COLL	Collins, Ellen, et al. *Tales of the Old Dutch Graveyard.* n.p.: The Heritage Committee, the Junior League of Westchester-on-Hudson, 1984.
CON	Conklin, Margaret Swancott. *Historical Tarrytown and North Tarrytown (A Guide).* Tarrytown, New York: The Tarrytown Historical Society, 1939.
COR	Cornell, et al. *A Primer of Ossining History.* Ossining, NY: Ossining Historical Society, 1984.
COU	Countryman, Edward. *A People in Revolution, The American Revolution and Political Society in New York, 1760-1790.* Baltimore & London: The Johns Hopkins University Press, 1981.
CR	Croke, Alice. Personal communication.
CRA	Crandell, Richard F. *This is Westchester.* Revised edition. New York: Sterling Publishing Company, 1961. [Originally published in 1954.]
CRO	*A Walker's Guide to The Old Croton Aqueduct.* Linda Gilbert Cooper, ed. New York State Office of Parks, Recreation and Historic Preservation, Taconic Region, in cooperation with the Lucius N. Littauer Foundation. Published in 1980s.
DA	*Tarrytown Daily News.*

DA2	*The Crash to VJ Day in the Tarrytowns of New York 1929-1945.* Verplank, NY: Historical Briefs, Inc., 1994. [Compilation of *Tarrytown Daily News* articles.]
DAN	Dankers, Jaspar and Peter Sluyter. *Journal of a Voyage to New York and a Tour in Several of the American Colonies in 1679-80.* Great Americana Series. Translated and edited by Henry C. Murphy. Brooklyn, 1867. n.p.: Readex Microprint Corp., 1966.
DAI	"Community Guide." n.p.: Gannett Suburban Newspapers, September 27, 1992.
DE	De Angelis, Vi[n]cent. *A Short History of the Town of Mount Pleasant New York Commemorating the 200th Anniversary of the Incorporation of the Town March 7, 1988.* n.p.: Rotary Clubs of Hawthorne, Pleasantville and Briarcliff Manor, 1988.
DI	*Dictionary of American Biography.* New York: Charles Scribner's Sons, 1936.
DU	Duboc, Jessie L. *In the Days of Ichabod.* Ann Arbor, Michigan: Edwards Brothers, Inc., 1939.
EA	East, Robert A. and Jacob Judd, eds. *The Loyalist Americans: A View From Greater New York.* Tarrytown, New York: Sleepy Hollow Restorations, 1976.
EW	Ewald, Captain Johann. *Diary of the American War, A Hessian Journal.* Joseph P. Tustin, trans. and ed. New Haven & London: Yale University Press, 1979.
FE	Fernow, B., ed. *Documents Relating to the History and Settlement of the Towns along the Hudson and Mohawk Rivers (with the Exception of Albany) from 1630-1684.* n.p.: Weed Parsons & Co., 1881.
FI	*First Record Book of the "Old Dutch Church of Sleepy Hollow" Organized in 1697 and now the First Reformed Church of Tarrytown, N. Y.* Rev. David Cole, D.D., trans. n.p.: The Yonkers Historical and Library Association, 1901.
FO	*Fourteen of Them.* With a foreword by Mary Roberts Rinehart. New York: Farrar & Rinehart, Inc., 1944.
GA	Gallagher, Frank. Personal communication, 9/15/94.]
GE	*Getting to Know the Tarrytowns.* Booklet, Sleepy Hollow Chamber of Commerce. Purdys, NY: MICA, Inc., 1995.
GET	*Getting to Know the Tarrytowns.* Booklet, Sleepy Hollow Chamber of Commerce. Purdys, NY: MICA, Inc., 1996.

GM	*GM Tarrytown, An Autobiography.* Tarrytown, NY: General Motors Corporation, 1996.
GR	Greene, Nelson, ed. *History of the Valley of the Hudson, River of Destiny, 1609-1930.* 5 volumes. Chicago: The S. J. Clarke Publishing Company, 1931.
HA	Hansen, Harry. *North of Manhattan.* New York: Hastings House, 1950.
HAD1	Hadaway, William, ed. *The McDonald Papers.* Part I. White Plains, N. Y.: Westchester County Historical Society, 1927.
HAD2	Hadaway, William, ed. *The McDonald Papers.* Part II. White Plains, N. Y.: Westchester County Historical Society, 1927.
HAN	*Handbook of North American Indians.* Vol. 15. Bruce G. Trigger, vol. ed. Washington, D.C.: Smithsonian Institution, 1978.
HAND	Hand, Julianna Free. *The Westchester Treasure Hunt Tour: Treason in the American Revolution.* Carole Breen, illust. Croton-on-Hudson, NY: Julianna Free Hand, 1980.
HAR	*Harper's New Monthly Magazine.*
HARP	*Harper's Weekly.* A modern reprint of Supplement, May 27, 1871.
HHV1	"Historic Hudson Valley, Sunnyside." n.p.: Historic Hudson Valley, n.d. Cover shows black and white photo, with orange field above.
HI	Hine, C. G. *The New York and Albany Post Road.* New York: C. G. Hine, 1905.
HIN	Hinton, Howard. *My Comrades, Adventures in the Highlands and Legends of the Neutral Ground.* New York: n.p., 1874.
HIS	*The Old Dutch Burying Ground of Sleepy Hollow.* n.p.: History Research Society of the Tappan Zee, 1926. [Very good for its highlights of many colonial lives.]
HIST	*Historical Magazine.* Vol. IX, no. 6. June 1865. pp. 179-180.
HISTOR	"Historical Society of the Tarrytowns." Brochure. n.p.: n.p., n.d. Printed blue on white paper, with 1927 map of the Hudson Valley.
HO	Howat, James K., ed. *The Hudson River and its Painters.* n.p.: American Legacy Press, 1983.

HU	Hutchinson, Lucille and Theodore Hutchinson. *The Centennial History of North Tarrytown.* n.p.: n.p., nd [1974].
HUF	Hufeland, Otto. *Westchester County during the American Revolution 1775-1783.* Harrison, New York: Harbor Hill Books, 1982. [A reprint of Hufeland's 1926 work.]
HUFE	Hufeland, Otto. *A Check List of Books, Maps, Pictures and other printed Matter relating to the Counties of Westchester and Bronx.* n.p.: Privately Printed, 1929.
HUT	Hutchinson, Lucille and Theodore. *Storm's Bridge: A History of Elmsford 1700-1976.* n.p.: Bicentennial Committee of Elmsford, 1980.
I1	"Philipse Manor Company to N.Y.C. & Hudson River R.R. Co.," May 9, 1912. Indenture in Westchester County Land Records Division.
IN	Ingersoll, Ernest. *Illustrated Guide to the Hudson River and Catskill Mountains.* Reprint, n.d. Originally published, 1910, J. C. & A. L. Fawcett, Inc.
IR	Irving, Washington. *The Selected Writings of Washington Irving.* Saxe Commins, ed. New York: The Modern Library, 1945.
IRVI	Irving, Washington. *The Sketch-Book of Geoffrey Crayon, Gent.* New York: A. L. Burt Company, n.d.
IRVIN	Irving, Washington. "Sleepy Hollow." *Miscellaneous Writings.* Volume II, 1803-1859. Wayne R. Kline, ed. Boston: Twayne Publishers, 1981. [In series, *The Complete Works of Washington Irving.* Henry Pochmann, general editor. Madison, Wisconsin: The University of Wisconsin Press, 1969.]
IRVING	Irving, Washington. *Sleepy Hollow, A Reminiscence Extracted from the Knickerbocker Magazine of May 1839.* North Tarrytown, NY: The Sleepy Hollow Society, 1993.
JA	Jameson, J. Franklin, Ph.D, LL.D. *Narratives of New Netherland.* Original Narratives of Early American History Series. New York: Barnes and Noble, 1937. [Originally published by Charles Scribner's & Sons, 1907.]
JAM	"History of the James House, Phelps Memorial Hospital Center, North Tarrytown, New York." Pamphlet. n.p.: n.p., n.d.

JE	Jenkins, Stephen. *The Greatest Street in the World.* New York: G. P. Putnam's Sons, The Knickerbocker Press, 1911.
KA	Kane, Florence. Director, Warner Library. Sleepy Hollow Society meeting 1995.
KE	Keller, Allan. *Life Along the Hudson.* Tarrytown, NY: Sleepy Hollow Restorations, 1976. [The oil painting of Upper Mills depicted on p. 231 appears very nearly contemporary with P4.]
LE	Lederer, Richard M., Jr. *The Place-Names of Westchester County New York.* Harrison, New York: Harbor Hill Books, 1978.
LO	Lossing, Benson. *The Hudson.* Reprint. Somersworth, New Hampshire: New Hampshire Publishing Co., 1972. [First published in book form 1866 by H. B. Nims & Co., Troy, NY. All or part of this work first appeared in the London *Art-Journal* during 1860 and 1861. The sketches can be considered to predate 1861.]
LOS	Lossing, Benson J. *The Pictorial Field-Book of the Revolution.* 2 vols. New York: Harper & Brothers, Publishers, 1851.
LYN	"Lyndhurst, Tarrytown, N. Y." A three-panel color brochure printed January, 1991.
M1	[Map.] Couzens, M. K. "Map of Part of the Manor of Philipsburgh in the County of Westchester NY Showing the Grants....Traced and reduced from fragments of the Original map..." Drawn and Compiled by M. K. Couzens...1880. New York Public Library, map division. [The rendering of the Post Road's Pocantico River crossing is not reliable.]
M2	[Map.] "Map of Westchester County New York From Actual Surveys by Sidney & Neff Civil Engineers and Surveyors." White Plains, New York: Newell S. Brown, 1851.
M3	[Map.] Travel map of Hudson River in booklet form. New York: A. T. Goodrich, 124 Broadway, N.Y.C., 1820. New York Public Library, map division.
M4	[Map.] A map of various grants showing "The Manor of Philips Burgh granted in 16[illegible], paying [pounds 4:12]..." New York Public Library, map division.

M5	[Map.] Burr, David H., "Map of the County of Westchester," Ithaca, New York: Stone & Clark, 1839. New York Public Library, map division.
M6	[Map.] "A Plan of the Manor of Philipsburg in the County of Westchester in the State of New York surveyed agreeable to the order and instructions of Isaac Stowsenbury & P. H. V. Cortlandt [Commissioners of Forfeiture] unto John Hill 1785. With the addition of the Southern end of Colen-Donck." New York Public Library, map division. [This is an important source. The map exhibits a considerable amount of damage through the areas of Tarrytown and Sleepy Hollow. However, it appears to be in several ways preferable to Couzens map which is not always precise. The Couzens map straightens out the distinctive "S" curve which the Albany Post Road made in passing the Old Dutch Church.]
M10	[Map.] Visscher, N. J. "Map of New Netherlands in 1655." In Van der Donck [VA].
M11	[Map.] Erskine, Robert. "General Contraction" [...of the Westchester County Area, 1778.] New York Historical Society, map collection.
M12	[Map.] Erskine, Robert. Survey of the Road Between Tarrytown and Croton River, c. 1778. [Erskine-Dewitt Map No. 12.] New York Historical Society, map collection.
M13	[Map.] Sauthier, Joseph Claude. "A Plan of the Operations of the King's Army... in New York...Engagement of the White Plains...." 1777. [Extremely inaccurate regarding locations of Tarrytown, White Plains, etc. Sing Sing is labeled Dobbs Ferry. There are far better contemporary maps of the area, although the Sauthier map may be the most widely published.]
M15	[Map.] *"Pays Situé entre Frog's Point et Croton River et position Des Armees American et Britannique[...] sur les Plaines Blanches."* [This appears to be a French version of a map in English, see M67.]
M16	[Map.] *"Position de L'armee American et Francaise a Philips-Bourg, distante de 12 Miles de Kingsbridge et 25 miles de New York depuis le 6 Juillet, 1781."* New York Historical Society, map collection.
M17	[Map.] Wiley, George. "Tarwe-town in the Manor of Phillipsburgh, Westchester Co. N.Y., 1781." This map

was prepared by Wiley for the publication of [AC] in 1899.

M18 [Map.] "Part of Village of Tarrytown." A reprint from a portion of Broomley's Atlas, distributed to local public school children in 1992 by Historical Society of the Tarrytowns.

M19 [Map.] "White Plains Quadrangle New York—Westchester Co." State of New York Department of Transportation from United States Department of the Interior Geological Survey, 1967. Photorevised 1979.

M20 [Map.] *Hagstrom Westchester Atlas.* 10th ed. Maspeth, NY: Hagstrom Map Company, 1984.

M21 [Map.] "Zoning map Village of North Tarrytown... Mayor Janet Gandolfo... Charles Riley, Licensed Land Surveyor." n.p.: n.p., n.d.

M22 [Map.] "Tarrytown immediately after the Revolution." [See TA.]

M28 [Map.] Cartwright, George W. "Map Showing the Proposed Bounds for the Incorporation of North Tarrytown Containing Two Square Miles by Geo. W. Cartwright C. E. Sing Sing 1874." n.p.: n.p., n.d. [See HU, p. 109.]

M29 [Map.] [Map of Tarrytown, 1926. See HISTOR.]

M30 [Map.] Erskine, Robert. "Scene of Operations before New York 1781." Survey, New York Historical Society, map collection.

M31 [Map.] Adams, William. "A Map of the Town of Greensburgh in the County of Westchester... by Wm Adams, 10CH: one inch." [Certified by Geo. Comb December 8, 1797. One unique feature of this map is the indication of early paths approximating present day Washington and Cortlandt Streets. See also M32.]

M32 [Map.] Adams, William. "A Map of the Town of Mount Pleasant in Westchester County by William Adams, Surveyor". [In Scharf's History of Westchester County [SC]. Scale of 40 chains = 1 inch indicated on the map. It appears that the map was prepared upon the founding of the township in 1788. According to Scharf, Adams was a surveyor and county supervisor from Mount Pleasant 1794-1797. He made maps of several of the townships. (See SC: vol. II, p.623.)]

M33 [Map.] Colles, Christopher. "From New York (9) to Poughkeepsie." [Published in 1789, but probably

	surveyed, by John Colles, during the time of the Revolution. In COL, p.129.]
M34	[Map.] "Map of the Beekman Farm Situated in the Town of Mount Pleasant... April 23rd 1848." Westchester Historical Society. [See HU, p. 57.]
M35	[Map.] Map of Tarrytown area in 1867 by Beers. Photocopy, Warner Library. See HU, p.84.
M36	[Map.] "Tarrytown Land Company." By Olmstead Vaux & Co. [1871] n.p.: n.p., n.d. [In the collection of the author.]
M37	[Map.] North Tarrytown in 1875. Sleepy Hollow Restorations Collection. See HU, p.181.
M38	[Map.] "Plan of Beekmantown Tarrytown and Irving, West Chester Co. N.Y. 20 rods to the inch." c. 1868. [In collection of the author. Many copies of this map are still in circulation.
M39	[Map.] Map of Westchester County. J. B. Beers & Co., 1881. [See BOL.]
M40	[Map. Tarrytown, North Tarrytown area in 1891. [See CA, p.220 and HU, p.179.]
M41	[Map.] North Tarrytown area in 1893. [See HU, p.157, credited to W. Arthur Slater Collection.]
M42	[Map.] North Tarrytown and Tarrytown area in 1897. [See BA.]
M43	[Map.] "Philipse Manor North Tarrytown Westchester Co. N.Y." Tarrytown, N.Y.: Wulff Engineering Co., October 10th, 1914. In Westchester County Land Records Division.
M44	[Map.] "Philipse Manor or Castle. North Tarrytown. Westchester County. N.Y., "Present Plot Plan." By C. Charbenneau, et al. June 1935. Westchester County Historical Society.
M45	[Map.] "New York Lower Westchester County Street and Road Map." New York: Geographia Map Co., 1979.
M47	[Map.] "Kaiser Handibook Map." [In Tarrytown phone book, 1987.]
M48	[Map.] "Zoning Map Village of North Tarrytown Town of Mount Pleasant Westchester County, New York." [Rey, August 8, 1974.] Charles Riley, Licensed Land Surveyor.

M49	[Map.] "Zoning Map Adopted January 17th, 1989, Village of Tarrytown Westchester County New York," Louise Camilliere, Village Clerk.
M50	[Map.] Adams, William. [A sketched survey of Mount Pleasant circa 1797, in HU, p.51. See note on M32.]
M51	[Map] Cartwright, Geo. W. "Map of the Village of Beekmantown North of Tarrytown... by Geo. W. Cartwright C. E." 1835. [In HU, p.53.]
M52	[Map.] Cartwright, Geo. W. "Map of the Village of Beekmantown... by Geo. W. Cartwright, C. E., Oct 1, 1836 1839." [In HU, p.54.]
M53	[Map.] "Hydrographic Map of the Counties of New York, Westchester, and Putnam, and also showing the line of the Croton Aqueduct." Lithograph by N. Currier, 152 Nassau Street, New York. [Appears to be a mid-19th Century map.]
M54	[Map.] "Preliminary Chart of the Hudson River New-York From Tellers Point to the Mouth...(1855)" (B No. 2.) [From "Survey of the Coast of the United States, A. D. Bache Superintendent of the survey." Shows clearly the limits of the bay at the Pocantico River's mouth.]
M55	[Map.] North Tarrytown area, c. 1818. [Credited to the collection of Arthur W. Slater in HU, p.45.]
M56	[Map.] "Plan of Tarrytown and Vicinity, 1870, Scale 20 rods to the inch." Displayed in Tarrytown Village Hall Examined, April, 1996].
M57	[Map.] Dorland, Mrs. Jack A. "Old Tarrytown (And Surrounding Area) 1788-1798." [A 20th century compilation from data provided by the Historical Society of the Tarrytowns.]
M58	[Map.] "Tarrytown, Irvington, North Tarrytown." Elmsford, NY: TransWestern Publishing, 1993.
M59	[Map.] Burr, David H. "Hudson River and Vicinity." New York: Disturnell (156 Broadway), 1835.
M60	[Map.] Wade, William. "Wade and Groome's Panorama of the Hudson River from New York to Albany." New York: Disturnell (102 Broadway), 1846.
M61	[Map.] "Map of the Hudson River from New York to Albany, Scale of 1 Mile to an Inch." Lith. G. Snyder 138 William St. NY [1848].
M62	[Map.] "Lloyd's Topographical Map of the Hudson River From the Head of Navigation at Troy to its confluence

	with the ocean at Sandy Hook [1864]." New York Public Library, map division.
M63	[Map.] Elmsford and East View in 1881. [See HUT, p.80.]
M64	[Map.] "Trails of the Rockefeller State Park Preserve Pocantico Hills, New York." A flyer giving trail names and lengths. n.p.: n.p., n.d.
M65	[Map.] "Map of North Tarrytown 1877." Scale, 150 feet per inch, Geo. L. Wiley & Bro. Surveyors, Tarrytown--June--1877. Sleepy Hollow Society collection. [Gift of Patricia Lawlor (d. 1996) a native North Tarrytown whose uncle had been a village engineer. The large map (approximately 78" wide) is in poor condition.]
M66	[Map.] Erskine, Robert. Westchester County. Copy in Ossining Historical Society collection. [Showing Tappan Creek, mile markers along Albany Post Road, Beaver Hill, etc.]
M67	[Map.] "A Plan of the Country from the Frog's Point to Croton River shewing the Positions of the American and British Armies from the 12th of October 1776 until the engagement on the White Plains on the 28th. Drawn by S. Lewis from the Original Surveys made by order of General Washington, and published in 1807. Reproduced, in 1885, to illustrate Dawson's Westchester County New York, during the American Revolution 1774-1783." [In Dawson, *Westchester County, New York, During the American Revolution*. Morrisania, New York: n.p., 1886.]
MA	MacDonald, John M. "The MacDonald Papers." Manuscript compilation of interviews conducted by John M. MacDonald. MacDonald's notes were transcribed by John English in the early 1860's. A photcopy of the manuscript with index are housed in the library of the Westchester Historical Society.
MI	Miller, Harry Edward. "In the Sleepy Hollow Country." *New England Magazine*. December 1900.
MO	Moran, Kathleen. *A Tour for Children in Beekmantown and North Tarrytown*. Edith S. Downing, illustr. Published for N. Tarrytown Centennial 1974. n.p.: n.p., n.d.
NE	*The New York Times*.

NEV	Nevins, Allan. *Study in Power, John D. Rockefeller.* 2 Volumes. New York & London: Charles Scribner's Sons, 1953.
NEW	*New York Times Obituary Index.*
NO	"North Tarrytown Recreation & Parks." Brochure sent to residents of village in September, 1994 describing recreational program.
NOR	"North Tarrytown Recreation & Parks." Brochure. Spring, 1996.
NORT	"Official Souvenir Program, Inspection Parade, North Tarrytown Fire Department, North Tarrytown, New York, September 4th, 1939."
OC	O'Callaghan, E. B., M.D., LL.D. *Documents Relative to the Colonial History of the State of New York Procured in Holland, England, and France By John Romeyn Broadhead, Esq. Agency*. Albany: Weed, Parsons & Co., 1854,1857, etc.
OE	Oechsner, Carl. *Ossining, New York, An Informal Bicentennial History.* n.p.: North River Press, Inc., 1975. [Prepared in cooperation with Ossining Bicentennial Celebrations, Inc.]
OW	Owens, William A. *Pocantico Hills 1609-1959.* Tarrytown, New York: Sleepy Hollow Restorations, 1960.
P1	[Picture.] "View of Carve's Mill, at Sleepy Hollow, Tarrytown, New York." *Gleason's Pictorial.* Vol. IV. No. 24—Whole No.102. Boston: Saturday, June 11, 1853. [Author's collection.]
P2	[Picture.] "Croton Aqueduct at Mill River." Lithograph: F. B. Tower, artist, W. Bennett, Sculptor [engraver]. n.p.: n.p., n.d. [Author's collection.]
P3	[Picture.] "View of the Old Dutch Church at Sleepy Hollow, New York." *Gleason's Pictorial.* Vol. IV. No.2—Whole No. 80. Boston: Saturday, January 8, 1853. [Author's collection.]
P4	[Picture.] "The Mill Pond, Sleepy Hollow, at Tarrytown, New York." *Gleason's Pictorial.* Vol. V. No.22—Whole No. 126. Boston: Saturday, November 26, 1853. [Author's collection.]
P5	[Picture.] "Tarrytown Institute, Tarrytown, New York." *Gleason's Pictorial.* 1853. [Author's collection.]
P6	[Picture.] "Sleepy Hollow Bridge, Tarrytown, New York." Reprinted from Lith. by Currier & Ives. [Note: imprints

	after 1857 read Currier & Ives, not N. Currier. [Author's collection.]
P7	[Picture.] "Sleepy Hollow Church, Near Tarrytown, N. Y." Reprinted from Lith. by N. Currier. Entered according to Act of Congress in the year 1867, by Currier & Ives, in the Clerk's Office of the district Court of the United States, for the Southern District of N.Y. [Author's collection.]
P8	[Picture.] A picture of the Old Dutch Church in Barber and Howe's Historical Collections..., 1842. *Heritage.* New York State Historical Association, March/April 1992. [Shows church just after portico was added.]
PA	Paulding, James Kirk. "The New Mirror for Travelers." *The Book of Vagaries.* New York: C. Scribner & Co., 1868. [Paulding first published this article in 1828.]
PE1	*New York History.* Cooperstown, NY: New York State Historical Association.
PE2	*Scenic Hudson News.* Poughkeepsie, NY, Scenic Hudson.
PEO	*People and the Parks, A History of Parks and Recreation in Westchester County.* A report. n.p.: n.p., n.d. [c.1985]
PH	"Philipse Manor-on-the-Hudson Westchester County, New York." Pamphlet. n.p.: n.p., n.d.
PHI	"Philipse Castle Restoration 1683-1785." Booklet. ["No.2 of a series of historical restorations published through the courtesy of Scalamandre Silks, Inc. (Second Edition)."] n.p.: n.p., n.d.
PHIL	"Philipsburg Manor Upper Mills." Brochure. n.p.: Historic Hudson Valley, n.d.
PHILI	*Philipsburg Manor.* Tarrytown, NY: Sleepy Hollow Restorations, 1969. [In the Ossining Public Library, 56 pp., paperback.]
RA	Raymond, Marcius D., comp. *Souvenir of the Revolutionary Soldiers' Monument Dedication.* Tarrytown, New York, 1894.
RAY	Raymond, Marcius D. *Washington at Tarrytown.* Tarrytown, NY: [Published by the author], 1893.
RAYM	Raymond, Marcius D. *David Williams and the Capture of André.* n.p.: n.p., n.d. [From a paper read before the Tarrytown Historical Society, January 15th, 1903.]
RO	Roe, Charles Harvey. *Historic Tarrytown Today.* Tarrytown, New York: The Tarrytown Press Record, February 1932.

RU	Ruttenber, E. M. *History of the Indian Tribes of Hudson's River.* Reprint. 2 vols. Saugerties, NY: Hope Farm Press, 1992. [Originally published in 1872.]
SA	Sargent, Winthrop. *Life and Career of Major John André.* William Abbatt, ed. New York: n.p., 1900. [Originally published by Ticknor & Fields, 1861.]
SC	Scharf, Thomas, J. *History of Westchester County, New York.* 2 vols., illust. Philadelphia: L. E. Preston and Co., 1886. [Entries regarding Greenburgh and Mount Pleasant contributed by Rev. John A. Todd, D. D., a former pastor of the Second Reformed Church, Tarrytown.]
SH	Shonnard, Frederic and W. W. Spooner. *History of Westchester County New York From its Earliest Settlement to the Year 1900.* Reprint. Harrison, New York: Harbor Hill Books, 1974. [Originally published by The New York History Company, 114 Fifth Avenue, New York in 1900.]
SL	"Sleepy Hollow Cemetery." [A revision of a 1905 pamphlet, currently being distributed by the cemetery. Includes a description of the cemetery and its founding c. 1905, and a map from about 1905.]
SM	Smith, Jack. Personal communication, 9/15/94.
ST	Steiner, Henry.
TA	*Tarrytown and the Tarrytown National Bank and Trust Company.* New York: n.p., 1932. [No author given, Charles Harvey Roe?]
TA2	*First English Record Book of the Dutch Reformed Church in Sleepy Hollow.* n.p.: The Tarrytown Historical Society, 1931. [Prepared for publication by Edgar Mayhew Bacon.]
TAP	*The Tappan Zee from the Half Moon to the Bridge.* Booklet, Tappan Zee Bridge Dedication Committee. [Copyright, 1955, Cort N. Palmer.]
TAR	*The Tarrytowns.* Tarrytown, New York: League of Women Voters, 1959.
TARR	Saberski, et al. *Tarrytown Centennial Album, Tarrytown Centennial 1870-1970.* Distributed during Tarrytown's village centennial. [Former Tarrytown historian, Wally Buxton (William C. Gross), appears to have been responsible for a great deal of the information in the album.]

TN	*Tarry News.* [Commenced publication in 1995. North Tarrytown, NY. Subsequently renamed, *Village News and Town Report.*]
TR	"A Century Given to God." Booklet. Tarrytown, NY: Church of the Transfiguration, 1995. [Issued as part of the church's centennial celebration in 1996.]
TW	*Two Hundred Fortieth Anniversary, 1697—1937, The First Reformed Church, Tarrytown New York.* "This is issued in response to a number of requests and is printed by order of the Consistory." n.p.: n.p., nd [1937].
TWO	*Two Hundredth Anniversary of the Old Dutch Church of Sleepy Hollow, October 10 and October 11, 1897.* Printed by The De Vinne Press for the Consistory of the First Reformed Church of Tarrytown, N. Y., 1898.
VA	Van Der Donck, Adriaen. *A Description of the New Netherlands.* Thomas F. O'Donnell, ed. Syracuse, New York: Syracuse University Press, 1968. [This is a modern edition of Jeremiah Johnson's 1841 translation of Van Der Donck's work. See VAN.]
VAN	vander Donck, Adriaen. *Beschryvinge Van Nieuw Nederlant.* n.p.: Aemsteldam, 1655. [New York Public Library, rare books collection.]
VAND	Van Doren, Carl. *The Secret History of the American Revolution.* New York: The Viking Press, 1941.
WA	*Washington Irving, Commemoration of the One Hundredth Anniversary of his Birth.* Washington Irving Association at Tarrytown-on-Hudson, Tuesday Evening, April 3, 1883. New York: G. P. Putnam's Sons, 1884.
WE	Wells, James L. *The Bronx and its People.* New York: Lewis Historical Publishing Co., 1927.
WES	*The Westchester Historian.* Quarterly of the Westchester Historical Society.
WESS	Wesselman, Piet. De Nederlandse Letteren, antiquarian bookseller, Amsterdam, Netherlands. Email, 4/20/96.
WEST	French, Alva P., ed. *History of Westchester County New York.* Will L. Clark, staff historian. New York & Chicago: Lewis Historical Publishing Co., 1925.
WI	Wilson, Rufus Rockwell. *Rambles in Colonial Byways.* 2 vols. Philadelphia: J. B. Lippincott Company, 1901.
WIL	Williams, J. L. *The Land of Sleepy Hollow and the Home of Washington Irving, a Series of Photogravure Representations, with Descriptive Letter-Press by J. L.*

	Williams. [Limited Letter-Press Edition.] New York: G. P. Putnam's Sons, The Knickerbocker Press, 1887. [Period photographs of Pocantico River Valley, historic sites, Sunnyside, and more. Greenburgh Library.]
WO	*Portrait of a Village, Wolfert's Roost, Irvington-on-Hudson.* Irvington-on-Hudson, New York: The Washington Irving Press, 1971.
WWW	*Who Was Who in America.*
YE	*Year of the Patriots, 1780-1980.* In Commemoration of The Three Captors of the British Spy, Tri-Village Bicentennial Irvington, North Tarrytown, Tarrytown. n.p.: n.p., n.d.
ZU	Zukowsky, John and Robbe Pierce Stimson. *Hudson River Villas.* New York: Rizzoli, 1985.

About the Author

Henry Steiner is the village historian of Sleepy Hollow, New York and a life-long resident of the two villages. He is a founder of the Sleepy Hollow Society and was a leader in the successful campaign to rename the Village of Sleepy Hollow, which gained international attention in 1996. An avid fly fisherman, he founded the Pocantico Fund in 1997 to help restore the historic Pocantico River as a trout stream.

Mr. Steiner is a director and producer of corporate communications for Northeast Video Productions. He has recently completed a historically annotated edition of Washington Irving's "The Legend of Sleepy Hollow" and is currently writing a collection of Sleepy Hollow stories and legends.

CPSIA information can be obtained at www.ICGtesting.com
Printed in the USA
BVOW04s1241120415

395789BV00014B/291/P